Cambridge Elements

Elements in Global China
edited by
Ching Kwan Lee
University of California, Los Angeles

GLOBAL CHINA'S SHADOW EXCHANGE

Tak-Wing Ngo
University of Macau

Shaftesbury Road, Cambridge CB2 8EA, United Kingdom

One Liberty Plaza, 20th Floor, New York, NY 10006, USA

477 Williamstown Road, Port Melbourne, VIC 3207, Australia

314–321, 3rd Floor, Plot 3, Splendor Forum, Jasola District Centre, New Delhi – 110025, India

103 Penang Road, #05–06/07, Visioncrest Commercial, Singapore 238467

Cambridge University Press is part of Cambridge University Press & Assessment, a department of the University of Cambridge.

We share the University's mission to contribute to society through the pursuit of education, learning and research at the highest international levels of excellence.

www.cambridge.org
Information on this title: www.cambridge.org/9781009486880

DOI: 10.1017/9781108975681

When citing this work, please include a reference to the DOI 10.1017/9781108975681

First published 2024

A catalogue record for this publication is available from the British Library.

ISBN 978-1-009-48688-0 Hardback
ISBN 978-1-108-97217-8 Paperback
ISSN 2632-7341 (online)
ISSN 2632-7333 (print)

Global China's Shadow Exchange

Elements in Global China

DOI: 10.1017/9781108975681
First published online: January 2024

Tak-Wing Ngo
University of Macau

Author for correspondence: Tak-Wing Ngo, twngo@um.edu.mo

Abstract: This Element shows China has assumed a historical role in shaping a new turn in globalization. It has assertively engaged in the open globalizing process through its Belt and Road Initiative as well as in the clandestine process through its shadow networks. These networks have incorporated millions of common people who are unwitting agents of transnational exchange in a global shadow economy. In contrast to the neoliberal phase, the shadow turn in globalization is driven by a plurality of individual, corporate, and state actors with unique divisions of labour, hierarchies of control and domination, and modes of operation. By virtue of being a nodal centre for shadow operations, China is exerting its shadow power in regrouping global city networks, redefining global value chains, and reconfigurating state borders and power.

Keywords: informal economy, global value chain, border governance, transnational networks, shadow globalization

ISBNs: 9781009486880 (HB), 9781108972178 (PB), 9781108975681 (OC)
ISSNs: 2632-7341 (online), 2632-7333 (print)

Contents

1 Introduction 1

2 The Global Shadow Economy 6

3 The Nodal Shadow Centre 18

4 Networks and Agents 34

5 Grey Governance in Shadow Globalization 53

6 Conclusion 64

References 67

1 Introduction

China's growing influence is shifting the global power structure. China is now the top exporting country and a key supplier in the global value chain. It has become a major investor in both the developed and the developing worlds. Its Belt and Road Initiative has mapped out an alternative geo-economic landscape that rivals neoliberal globalization. By deploying policy tools in economic statecraft, China is gaining international dominance through its market leverage, loans, and investment strategies. It is developing sharp power by fostering clientelist relationship with developing countries, and has been earnestly nurturing its soft power through cultural engagement, media communication, education, and overseas exchange.

While there is much debate on China's rising dominance in the global economy and its impact on the world order, its concomitant leverage in the global shadow economy remains underexamined. This is hardly surprising because the shadow economy itself has received only scant attention. But the fact is that globalization has increased the transnational flow of resources not only in terms of recorded trade, FDI, migration, and information but also unregulated or unrecorded products and services exchanged in shadow. These shadow operations range from smuggling, drug trafficking, illegal immigration, and money laundering to counterfeit trade and suitcase trade in daily consumables such as cigarettes, mobile phones, clothing, and foodstuff.

The shadow links hidden within the long supply chains are often innovative and unnoticeable. As such, tons of fresh seafood such as Australian lobster, Japanese abalone, and Norwegian salmon served in Chinese restaurants are flown in every day from their places of origin to Taiwan, Hong Kong, and Vietnam before being smuggled into mainland China for diners. Sweaters and trousers sold at New York stores are first made in the southern Chinese city of Dongguan, distributed on a large scale at wholesale outlets in Yiwu, delivered to the Dongxing border, smuggled in batches to Móng Cái in Vietnam, and then reassembled in Hanoi for export to the United States after 'Made in Vietnam' labels are attached to the items of clothing. In essence, the shadow economy is far more omnipresent and integral to our daily life than we realize.

Compared to its use of sharp power and soft power, China's leverage in this informal, underground process constitutes a kind of 'shadow power' that has hitherto been largely overlooked. Although piecemeal research has underlined China's predominant share in counterfeiting and money laundering practices around the world, an overview of China's position in the global shadow economy is absent. This is an omission that should be rectified in light of the global scale of shadow exchange. In fact, such shadow activity has more far-reaching penetration than mainstream globalization by virtue of its expansion into the once-marginalized regions of the world.

In particular, China is a driving force in one type of exchange that is becoming the dominant form of operation in the global shadow economy. So far shadow exchange has often been seen from two ends. One end is investigated by criminologists and international political economists who focus on transnational criminal groups with their highly organized and secretive operations in drug smuggling, human trafficking, arm trade, organ transplant, money laundering, and other transnational crimes. The other end is studied by anthropologists researching the small-scale, informal trade carried out by petty smugglers who shuttle daily consumables across state borders. In between the two ends, the middle spectrum remains largely unexplored. This middle spectrum is characterized by shadow exchanges that are connected, transnational in nature, and large in scale. Yet these exchanges differ from the secretive transnational crimes in that they involve a large number of people and are profoundly visible. They also stand apart from the discrete, petty smuggling activities through their deep embedment in the formal economy and incorporation into the global system of exchange. This embedded shadow exchange involving masses of people is closely linked to global China.

In order to fully apprehend China's unique position in the global shadow economy, we must historicize this economic activity. From a longue durée perspective, shadow exchanges such as smuggling, trafficking, and money laundering are nothing new, having been a part of human activities since time immemorial. Under trade restrictions and tax differences, goods can leave with one value on one side of a state boundary and arrive on the other side with a different value. Contrived profit induced by state control creates the economic incentive for smugglers to engage in shadow exchanges, even at the risk of being penalized. Historians have highlighted the central role played by merchants, peddlers, and traders who expanded trade and commerce over long distances through both licit and illicit means in laying the foundation for the emergence of modern capitalism (Braudel 1992). The question is that if shadow exchange is a perennial activity driven by market demand, what is the peculiarity of contemporary shadow exchange that accords a special role to global China?

Illicit trade dating back several centuries has been rampant in advanced countries and developing regions alike. Shadow activities were constitutive of diverse communities in the Mediterranean (Horden and Purcell 2000), the Sahara (Scheele 2012), the Arabian Sea (Mathew 2016), and many others. In America, illicit trading networks were built by British merchants after the discovery of the New World in defiance of official mercantilist control, linking colonial ports to the West Indies and continental Europe (Andreas 2013). Likewise, in Latin America, European traders created a shadow economy parallel to the official system that was based on smuggling, corruption, and fraud of all kinds (Bailyn 2005). In the Middle East, merchants and smugglers mobilized their diasporic networks to evade regulations and organized their operations flexibly to find profitable niches (Mathew 2016). In maritime Southeast Asia, the smuggling of drugs, arms, people, and currency went hand in hand with the construction of borders in the British and Dutch colonies during the second half of the nineteenth century (Tagliacozzo 2005). In mainland Southeast Asia, Laotian and Chinese traders created extensive illicit networks to circumvent French regulations aimed at diverting trade from Siam to Vietnam (Walker 1999). In Japan, a huge shadow economy emerged after WWII to encompass not only smuggling, drug trafficking, and money laundering but also such activities as underground gambling and Internet dating (Mizoguchi 2016).

In China, shadow exchange has left a lasting imprint on the country's modern history. Opium was smuggled by Britain into the Qing empire during the nineteenth century to generate revenue for the Crown. The Qing government's attempt to ban the trafficking led to the Opium Wars. China's defeat resulted in the ceding of Hong Kong to Britain, which precipitated the historical issue about Hong Kong's return to China in 1997. During the Republican period, the Chinese maritime customs already uncovered elaborate and organized networks of shadow trading, linking regional merchants with distant suppliers. These shadow traders took complicated land and sea routes to escape the attention of the customs authorities. They secured deposits from boatmen as collateral, paid protective tributes to pirates, and bribed local officials. In some extreme cases, organized gangs and even whole communities were involved in the trafficking of narcotics, weapons, and consumer commodities. Some smugglers even built wireless stations to coordinate their operations as well as to monitor official actions (Thai 2018: 119–120, 138). Later on, opium smuggling was carried out by the Chinese Communist Party during the Yan'an period. Revenue from the opium trade was used to finance the revolution and to develop the Shaan-Gan-Ning area under communist control (Chen 1995).

Shortly after WWII, gold bullion was airlifted from Manila, Bangkok, Saigon, Rangoon, and Calcutta to Hong Kong and then transported to Macao. By 1948, Macao had imported more gold than any other market in the world, the majority of which was further smuggled into China (Thai 2018: 238). But most intriguing of all was the role played by the Kowloon–Canton Railway, which served as a smuggling artery in the Pearl River Delta as well as a connecting gateway to the Guangzhou–Hankow Railway that reached central China.

At various locales, passengers would throw overboard their cargo, including bulky commodities such as rice and flour, from a moving train to fellow carriers waiting along the rail track. The picked-up cargoes would be distributed to nearby towns and villages. The whole operation was facilitated by train operators who adjusted the train speed when loading or unloading was done at specific spots along the train journey (Thai 2018: 234–5).

After the outbreak of the Korean War and the subsequent UN embargo against China, smuggling became a means for China to offset the pressure of Western sanctions. Hong Kong, and to a lesser extent Macao, served as the primary base for such state-sponsored shadow exchange as well as the source of foreign currencies. The United States estimated that each month some 5,000 tons of goods were smuggled into China and Macao via Hong Kong in 1952 (Zhang 2001: 321, n22). During the same period, over 90 per cent of Hong Kong exports to Macao were re-exported to mainland China. Although Western nations were aware of the trade leakage to China through shadow channels, they turned a blind eye to the situation lest strict restrictions would severely damage the Hong Kong economy, which carried the risks of mass unrest and the communist takeover of Hong Kong (Zhang 2001: 36–41).

These are examples of deeply rooted transnational shadow exchange throughout modern history. More importantly, it is closely linked to modern state building. For instance, illicit trade played a part in the American Revolution when colonial smugglers made use of their existing shadow networks and knowledge to supply the insurgency. American industrialization was also facilitated by smuggled machinery and trafficked workers with labour skills and expertise (Andreas 2013: 14–15 and 45). Yet the role of shadow exchange in modern state building is not only functional but also institutional. The development of state borders was intimately linked with smuggling activities that sought to subvert borders. In essence, boundary production and boundary transgression are two sides of the same coin. The relationship appears like a 'waltz' between the state and smugglers, where each measure is met with a countermeasure, prompting the adoption of new measures in a new cycle (Tagliacozzo 2005: 373). In this game of waltz, modern states have earnestly developed infrastructural power to extend their despotic reach to the margins. Eventually, the measures to curb smuggling by means of tightening control of borders, improvement in revenue collection, and greater uniformity in regulations have become the building blocks of the modern state (Thai 2018: 10).

Because of that, some observers have warned against overstating the contemporary novelty of shadow exchanges at the expense of historical significance (Karras 2010). At most, illicit globalization is the continuation of a centuries-old tradition in human civilization (Andreas 2013). This warning is well taken. However, if smuggling and trafficking have been integral to the modern state system and the global economy, how does the current pattern differ from the past? What role does global China play in this changing pattern?

Some researchers have highlighted the onset of virtual connectivity and cybercrimes as the distinctive feature of shadow exchange in our time (Shelley 2018). Online black market sites such as Silk Road, Farmer's Market, and Black Market Reloaded have vastly expanded the platform for illicit transactions in drugs, child pornography, stolen credit cards, and weapons. Other researchers have underlined the emergence of global shadow networks in criminal alliances, partnerships, and coordination mechanisms (Strange 1996; Castells 1998; Mandel 2010; Sharman 2011), although they differ in their assessment of the organizational strength of these global criminal networks. For instance, whereas Shelley (2014) argues that transnational crime, corruption, and terrorism can no longer be analysed separately since they are linked together in a globalized world, Andreas (2004) believes that criminal organizations have flattened out, dispersed, and become more network-oriented to escape crackdown under intensified law enforcement pressure.

Alongside the highly organized transnational criminal groups, contemporary shadow exchange is also carried out by ordinary people organized around flexible networks. Compared to its historical counterparts, smuggling is now no longer an activity undertaken exclusively by professional traders or criminal gangs. Instead, hundreds of thousands of ordinary people are engaging in illicit trade on a daily basis. Such mass smuggling has been observed in different parts of the world and has been studied in various case-specific research (for instance, Fedorova 2012; Ayimpam 2015; Koff 2015; Elsing 2019; Fehlings 2022). These activities are seen to be undertaken by small-scale, loosely organized actors operating in isolation, forming a global mosaic of informal exchange.

While these findings are novel and informative, they have glossed over a major group of shadow activities that is becoming the dominant form of global shadow exchange. This group consists of a wide range of loosely connected shadow exchanges that are situated in between the transnational crimes undertaken by criminal organizations and the petty smuggling by solitary traders. These shadow exchanges are well embedded in the global economy and are parts of value chains that link domestic and transnational transactions on a global scale. Many legal commodities as well as counterfeits, knockoffs, and forbidden items are integrated into long chains of production and distribution across nations. In other words, there is a substantial overlapping between this shadow sector and the open economy. Shadow exchanges are no longer confined to black markets or exclusively carried out by organized criminal groups.

Instead, a large number of legitimate market players, including individuals as well as corporate and institutional actors, take part in both open and shadow activities (Hall 2012).

This embedded shadow sector of the global mass is unique in history. As our subsequent discussion will show, this sector develops in tandem with the rise of global China. China provides the market platform, infrastructural support, and active agency that facilitate the growth of this embedded shadow sector. In return, the shadow sector enhances China's global expansion and forges a new turn in globalization that has become China-centred. A close study of the universe of this shadow economy will therefore add to our understanding of global China and its shadow power.

2 The Global Shadow Economy

In order to understand how global China and shadow exchange have become mutually constitutive, it is imperative to have some basic idea about the global shadow economy and the nature of transnational shadow exchange. However, this is not straightforward, not only because of the clandestine nature of shadow exchange that makes it hard to observe and document but also because of its conceptual ambiguity. Some of the controversies are discussed here with a view to highlight the theoretical insights that enable us to analyse China's shadow exchange. The discussion also underlines the ways which the China case in turn contributes to our understanding of the global shadow economy.

Shadow Exchange on a Global Scale

To begin with, what are the scale and scope of the global shadow economy? Unfortunately, even though shadow exchange is believed to have reached a massive scale, a precise estimation of its scope is difficult because of its clandestine nature. Measuring something that is not recorded is indeed very challenging. While informed guesses abound, they are subject to criticism.

From the outset, the lack of an agreed definition and categorization means that estimations vary significantly, depending on how broad or narrow the definition is. This is compounded by different measurement and calculation methods. Measurement techniques include direct surveys of shadow activities, statistical models, and the use of macroeconomic indicators (such as tax audits, currency demand, unemployment rate, and so on). Notwithstanding complex econometric computations, none can claim to be problem-free in their estimations. Different methods generate findings with varying margins. Even the same method has compatibility issues in cross-country comparison because of differences in definition and questionnaire design.

Notwithstanding substantial variations, all existing estimations point to the fact that shadow exchange is anything but marginal in the domestic and global economies. For instance, in a recent report, OECD/ILO (2019) estimates that two billion people, representing 61 per cent of the global working population, work in the shadow, informal sector. In developing and emerging countries, 70 per cent of workers are in informal employment. The report concludes that informality is the norm in developing countries.

By far the most ambitious estimation is by Schneider and Williams (2013), who tried to gauge the size of the shadow economy in 162 countries with the help of econometric models. They found that in 2007, the shadow economy constituted some 16 per cent of the total GDP in 162 countries worldwide. In terms of country breakdown, the size of the shadow economy was 13 per cent of the GDP for the OECD countries, 26 per cent for developing countries, and 34 per cent for transition countries. Bolivia had the largest shadow economy (66.1 per cent of the national income), followed by Georgia (65.8 per cent), Panama (63.5 per cent), Zimbabwe (61.8 per cent), Azerbaijan (58 per cent), and Peru (58 per cent). The smallest shadow economies were found in Switzerland (8.5 per cent), the United States (8.6 per cent), Luxembourg (9.7 per cent), Austria (9.8 per cent), Japan (11 per cent), United Kingdom (12.5 per cent), and, surprisingly, China (12.7 per cent).

In terms of commodity exchange, Naim (2005: 112) quotes an INTERPOL report warning that trade in counterfeits has grown eight times the increase in legitimate trade since the early 1990s. Similarly, the OECD warns that global trade in counterfeit goods has increased steadily in the past three decades, rising from 1.9 per cent of global trade in 2007 to 2.5 per cent in 2017 and further to 3.3 per cent in 2019 (OECD/EUIPO 2016). Commercial losses around the world due to counterfeiting were estimated to be around USD500 billion in the 2000s, compared to USD5 billion twenty years ago, with the cost of counterfeiting between 5 per cent and 10 per cent of the total value of world trade.

In terms of human smuggling, a UN report indicates that at least 2.5 million migrants were smuggled in 2016 globally, earning human smugglers an income of up to USD7 billion (UNODC 2018). These were people who migrated voluntarily by shadow means. Another twenty million people were trafficked worldwide, most of whom ended up in child labour, forced labour, or sex labour (ILO 2017).

The most prominent source of shadow exchanges can be found in shadow banking and the global money chain. One report (Shen 2016: 2) estimates that on the eve of the 2008 global financial crisis, the size of shadow banking was USD20,000 billion, almost twice the size of the formal banking system

(USD11,000 billion). The size of shadow banking assets accounted for nearly 120 per cent of the global GDP at that time. Shadow banking in China during the early 2010s was estimated to be around CNY20–30 trillion (USD3–4.5 trillion), making it the world's third biggest shadow banking sector after the United States and the United Kingdom (Shen 2016: 3).

In the global circulation of shadow capital, recent leaks (including the Luxembourg tax files in 2014, HSBC files in 2015, Panama Papers in 2016, and Paradise Papers in 2017) reveal the astounding wealth hidden in offshore tax havens. Studies by Zucman (2013) and Harrington (2016) alert us to the existence of a professional business sector that organizes the global shadow money chain. In a 2013 report, Global Financial Integrity estimated that global cumulated illicit financial outflows amounted to USD5.9 trillion in the period between 2002 and 2011. China was the biggest exporter of illicit capital, with a cumulation of USD1.08 trillion, followed by Russia, Mexico, Malaysia, and India (Kar and LeBlanc 2013).

Problems with these estimations abound. Besides the opaque nature, other factors such as the lack of reliable data, the ambiguity in classification, and the extremely wide range of shadow activities also make a realistic estimation tenuous, if not impossible. A former economist for the UN cautions that UN statistics on the global drug trade is often based on guesswork and exaggeration and should be treated with great caution (Thoumi 2005). Andreas (2011) thus warns against falling prey to a politics of numbers that is susceptible to speculation, distortion, and even fabrication. A good case in point is Schneider and Williams's (2013) calculation of China's shadow economy, the size of which was reported to be one of the smallest in the world. This questionable finding casts serious doubt on their estimations.

The aim here is therefore not to assess the accuracy of different estimations or to offer alternative calculations. Rather, the goal is to obtain a glimpse of the magnitude of shadow exchanges in the contemporary period. Notwithstanding the debatable estimations, one can safely conclude that although illicit exchanges have been a part of human activities since time immemorial, their scale and scope are unprecedented at the present time. This prompts Nordstrom (2000: 38) to argue that if shadow exchanges collapse overnight, the world economy will be in chaos.

Causes of the Shadow Expansion

There are many arguments and debates about the global expansion of the shadow economy. At the risk of oversimplification, these various accounts can be classified as functional, institutional, and structural. The functional argument emphasizes the marginality and peripherality of shadow activities associated with the urban poor. The informal economy arose in response to unemployment, bureaucratic red tape, and the liminality of the poor (Priest 1994; de Soto 2000; Centeno and Portes 2006; Perry et al. 2007). In this line of argument, informality is seen as a survival strategy of locals in response to their exclusion from the formal market (see Pohit and Taneja 2000; Walther 2009; Njikam and Tchouassi 2011). Informality functions as an economic safety net (Gershuny 1979; Pahl 1988; Maloney 2004) that provides employment opportunities for migrants (Portes and Bach 1985; Waldinger and Lapp 1993; Tienda and Raijman 2000). In the words of Anderson and Gerber (2008: 128), the informal sector serves multiple functions as a survival strategy for the poor; provider of jobs; training ground for underprivileged entrepreneurs; source of new businesses; and as a cost-reducing strategy for indigenous businesses.

Although the functional argument remains popular, its one-sidedness has become increasingly apparent in light of shadow activities proliferating in rich countries. The characterization of informality as the domain of the poor becomes problematic because many informal activities are generating relatively high levels of profit and are becoming part and parcel of economic life in both rich and poor countries (Castells and Portes 1989; Koff 2015). In response, some observers have shifted to an institutional argument that focuses on the strength and weakness of the regulatory state. Kus (2010) observes that the size of the informal economy tends to be largest in nations with highly regulated rules that are weakly enforced, and smallest where regulatory laws are limited but effectively enforced. In a similar vein, Eilat and Zinnes (2002) argue that shadow activities are most obvious in transitional economies where weak or dysfunctional governance mechanisms fail to effectively regulate economic exchanges. Arguing from a slightly different angle, students of borderland studies emphasize either the weakness of state power in border regions or argue that peripheral authorities tolerate smuggling in deliberate defiance of central policies (Cornelius 2004).

While the institutional account is convincing when analysing shadow exchange within a country, it has limitations with regard to transnational operations where smugglers arrange their shadow transactions across multiple nations whose institutional strength vary. In fact, as will be shown in the subsequent discussion, institutional strength is at best uneven at different border checkpoints (as well as at different time periods) even within a single country. Although institutions matter in facilitating or inhibiting shadow exchange, institutions alone cannot serve as a full explanation about the unprecedented expansion of shadow exchange on a global scale, unless we are prepared to conclude that from a historical point of view, contemporary state institutions are at their weakest.

The third line of argument underlines the changing structure of contemporary capitalism in driving the expansion of shadow exchanges. In other words, the contributing factors derive not from the domestic circumstances of individual countries but from macro historical processes. Viewing from this vantage point, Portes and Sassen-Koob (1987) suggest that falling profits as a result of increasing labour costs and competition from foreign goods have made informalization attractive. Informalization allows firms to attain flexible production, profit generation, and cost reduction in post-Fordist times. Hung and Ngo (2019) highlight the bridging role of the informal economy when corporate capitalism fails to deliver goods through the global commodity chain. Sassen (2006) argues that the decline of the manufacturing-dominated industrial complex of the post-war era and the rise of a new service-dominated economic complex have contributed to the rise of informalization.

In a more eclectic analysis, Shelley (2018) highlights a number of contemporary developments – including the increase in global competition, mobility of resources, decline of borders, and technological progress, especially the rise of the Internet and social media – in contributing to the growth of shadow exchanges. These are further compounded by population growth, expansion of the middle class, the emergence of transitional economies, and the rise of transnational criminals and terrorists in creating unprecedented supply and demand for shadow products. In particular, technology is a key driver of illicit trade. Such an activity endures because states, companies, and powerful individuals profit from it (Shelley 2018: 205–9).

The structural argument offers the most convenient point of departure to investigate transnational shadow exchange. It reminds us that the apparently discrete, unrelated shadow operations in different parts of the world are in fact driven by more general historical contingencies relating to the changing structure of global production, consumption, and distribution. While domestic economic conditions, liminality of the poor, and institutional weakness may be conducive to the growth of shadow exchanges in individual countries, the ubiquity of such operations across continents hinges upon broader historical and structural factors in the world economy.

Here the structural jigsaw is incomplete without acknowledging the role of global China. Informalization in post-Fordist production and distribution is more attractive when global value chains become more diverse, flexible, and, most important of all, intricately linked to shadow operations. Put differently, many shadow exchanges are no longer isolated activities operating at random but are integrated into global value chains that benefit not only the poor but also established firms, multinationals, and states. The creation and operation of such open-cum-shadow value chains is possible because of the existence of nodal centres that coordinate this new process. China is one of the centres.

Different Shades of Grey

Before looking at China's role in the global shadow exchange, we must clarify what shadow exchange entails. Defining shadow exchange immediately opens a can of worms. The problems include the wide range of clandestine activities, the shifting meanings of illicitness and the arbitrary nature of such shifts, as well as the epistemological challenge to the common understanding of the economic.

From the outset, numerous labels have been used to describe such activities: shadow, hidden, informal, parallel, underground, grey, black, illicit, illegal, and clandestine. Their defining feature, as observers point out, is their existence outside government record (Fleming et al. 2000: 387). Unfortunately, other than this common but broad denominator, a precise definition does not seem tenable. According to some economists, shadow exchanges entail economic activities that escape government accounting, taxation, and observation (Smith 1997; Fleming et al. 2000; Dell'Anno and Schneider 2003). The problem with this benchmarking of unrecorded goods and services based on government accounting and taxation is that it creates a very broad definition. Besides obvious criminal activities such as smuggling, trafficking, prostitution, money laundering, illegal gambling, and counterfeiting, this definition also includes housework, mutual help, street hawking, unregistered freelancing, moonlighting, barter exchange, gleaning, and scavenging, to name a few.

Even when the definition is narrowed down, there is still a plurality of activities that differ substantially in their operations. For instance, Schneider and Williams (2013) adopt a narrow definition to include only the production of legal goods and services that are deliberately concealed from public authorities. They also exclude all voluntary household work. Under this narrow definition, the kinds of shadow exchanges are reduced substantially, but still include diverse activities such as street hawking, suitcase trading, tax-evading practices, freelancing and moonlighting, and all kinds of informal work.

Criminologists and political scientists, on the other hand, tend to define and categorize shadow exchanges in terms of the legality and formality of the goods and practices involved. Very often, a shades-of-grey taxonomy is used, under which shadow activities are categorized according to the degree of illicitness (cf. Nordstrom 2000: 39). This ranges from dark exchanges involving illegal and dangerous goods (such as drugs and weapons), as well as illegal and immoral practices (human trafficking), to deep grey exchanges in illegal but non-dangerous goods (such as endangered animal products, counterfeits, and stolen goods), medium grey exchanges in legal commodities through illicit channels (such as cigarettes and taxable items, money), and light grey exchanges in legal commodities through informal practices (such as clothing, food, and daily consumables, by means of suitcase trading and crowd smuggling). In general, the darker the operations, the more covert the transactions (Ngo and Hung 2019: 183).

The problem with this shades-of-grey taxonomy is that although it is conceptually distinguishable, the actual practice is anything but clear-cut. Clandestine activities are most often undertaken in mixed forms. Drugs, animal parts, and ordinary foodstuff are often transacted through the same trading network. A suitcase trader will put counterfeit goods together with normal consumables to pass customs control. Different shades-of-grey operations do not work in isolation but take place in conjunction, making any clear distinction meaningless.

Yet diversity is only one of the problems. Another major issue is the shifting meaning of illicitness. In essence, the different shades of grey are anything but ontologically predefined. Far from it, the legality and illegality of goods and services can be said to be arbitrarily classified, mainly by state power. The state, past and present, holds absolute power to name what activities are illicit and which commodities are prohibited. Throughout human history, prohibited goods have included not only hazardous items such as opium, weapons, animal parts, and precious metals but also consumables such as salt, sugar, cigarette, molasses, herbs, rayon, and kerosene, to name a few. Trading in salt and sugar was once as heavily penalized as trading in drugs. In short, the transaction of what products at which periods are classified as illegal and dangerous is at best arbitrary and temporal. It depends entirely on state policies, which vary across time and space. Because of that, open and shadow activities – or formal and informal activities – do not exist in isolation and do not function independently of each other. Instead, they are mutually embedded, with a high degree of fluidity between them (Koster and Smart 2019). Many trading activities are formal and informal, as well as legal and illegal, at the same time, making bipolar categories problematic (Galemba 2008).

A further complication about the meaning of illicitness is that in modern times, almost all activities relating to the production of material value are under state control, surveillance, and regulation. The state oversees every single step and process in the chain of production, circulation, and consumption. This totalization process results in economic formalization, where every single transaction involving the creation or exchange of material value is recorded and hence regulated. Any activity that does not follow state-sanctioned rules of transaction is excluded from the realm of economics by definitional fiat. The idea of the informal, shadow, or underground economy essentially becomes a dumping ground for any activity that falls outside this epistemic understanding. Such activities, considered at best marginal and pathological, are meant to be eliminated. It is, according to Gibson-Graham (2006), a hegemonic discourse in which formal economic exchange is seen as the only legitimate form of material transaction.

These diverse understandings reveal the difficulty in giving a conclusive definition to shadow exchange. Instead of engaging in a futile attempt to arrive at a definitive understanding, this study will underline the conceptual ambiguities to locate the rich variety of shadow forms and operations. We borrow insights on informality from Castells and Portes (1989) to define shadow exchange broadly as a specific relationship of production and exchange of marketable material value that is unregulated by the state or other formal institutions. It includes a broad array of operations in different shades of grey, but excludes such activities as housework, community service, and mutual help that involve little or no tradable value. And unlike recent works by criminologists who focus on organized crimes such as human trafficking, theft, animal poaching, drug trade, illegal logging, bank fraud, cyber hacking, and terrorism, the subsequent discussion mainly deals with the exchange of tangible goods and money across state borders as the most common forms of mass smuggling. As mentioned in Section 1, this kind of shadow exchange is peculiar to our time.

Furthermore, despite its imprecise nature, the term 'shadow' is still preferred to other terms such as illicit, underground, or grey, which imply criminality. It also bears less binary connotation than the term 'informal', which is often defined in opposition to the formal sector. In brief, a more common term is used expediently here to engage with a broad audience before new vocabularies gain currency (Ngo 2015: 47).

It should be noted that although shadow exchange implies that the activity is opaque, it does not mean that it is therefore hidden. Quite the contrary, many such activities are conducted in the open and in broad daylight. It is opaque mainly in the sense that the activity is not recorded in any official metrological entry (Mitchell 2008) nor does it follow standardized 'accountics' in measuring and expressing economic activities (Suzuki 2007a, 2007b). These supposedly opaque activities are carried out in the open because they are tacitly tolerated. Paradoxically, notwithstanding the desire of the modern state to control all exchanges of material value, governments often tolerate ostensibly forbidden activities, especially when criminalization bears worse consequences if efforts to suppress fail (Heyman and Smart 1999). This ambiguity creates room for flexibility and indeterminacy that allows for mutuality and plasticity in regulatory governance. This apparent irony will be fully illustrated in the subsequent discussions.

State Borders and Border Crossing

Another key issue in transnational shadow exchange is the nature of state borders. Ironically, politically constructed borders aiming to exclude unwanted people and goods actually help generate such unwanted flows. This is because trade restrictions and border control create relative scarcity, hence the demand for restricted goods and services. Such a demand provides the incentive for shadow traders to engage in cross-border smuggling. It is in this sense that Newman and Paasi (1998) emphasize the connectivity function rather than the exclusion function of borders.

While state borders appear universal, the concept of borders has been under critical scrutiny in recent years. The Westphalian idea of sovereign states with clear and demarcated territorial borders has been criticized for its conceptual fixity. Contrary to such fixity, the legal/political boundary of a state border is often incongruent with the living socio-economic boundary. In many borderlands, social communities that cut across the political divide imposed by territorialized borders were already in place prior to the formation of the modern nation state or before the reification of state borders. In the wake of such incongruence, borders are at best soft and porous. Interactions among networks of kinship, clanship, and cultural partnership continue despite the imposition of political boundaries, constituting a kind of 'transboundary social formation' (Herzog 1990: 135).

In this regard, China is an exemplary case of soft borders despite its hard-line stand on territorial sovereignty. China is a direct neighbour of fourteen sovereign states, making it the country that shares the most borders with other countries in the world. In addition, China's maritime border is shared with half a dozen East and Southeast Asian countries. Some of these borders are exceedingly long and fragile. Notwithstanding strict customs regimes at its official border checkpoints, the Chinese state has difficulty in manning border traffic. Take Yunnan province for example. It alone shares a total land border of 4,060 km with Myanmar, Laos, and Vietnam. It has eight border cities, twenty-five border counties, nineteen national ports, six provincial ports, sixty-five border passages, and countless pathways, rivers, and sewage tunnels connected to the three neighbouring countries. In such circumstances, maintaining a rigid border is at best a myth.

Before the outbreak of Covid-19, extensive cross-border exchanges and human mobility took place every day. Controlling this huge volume of activities has proven to be beyond the capacity of the Chinese state. This is seen in all regions bordering other countries, including Myanmar, Vietnam, Kazakhstan, Korea, Russia, and Mongolia. Cross-border activities particularly abound in border communities such as Ruili (Sino-Burmese border), Huoerguosi (Sino-Kazakh border), and Yanbian (Sino-Korean border), where ethnic social formations have existed long before political boundaries were drawn. As a matter of fact, when the Chinese government closed its borders in response to the Covid-19 pandemic, the volume of undocumented migration soared in all border towns, resulting in a 90 per cent increase in prosecuted cases in 2020, which reveals the gap between the rhetoric of border maintenance and the actual daily life in borderlands (Baud and van Schendel 1997).

In addition to being soft and porous, borders are increasingly seen as diffused and fluid (Balibar 2002). They are by no means always located at the edge or periphery. Dry ports, free trade zones, and special economic regions are good examples. Borders have become mobile and multifaceted, with overlapping loyalties (Beck 2000). Furthermore, the advancement of e-commerce, Internet banking, platform logistics, and so on renders conventional territorial and physical boundaries increasingly obsolete. Radical critics such as Parker and Vaughan-Williams et al. (2009: 583) claim that borders are 'increasingly ephemeral and/or impalpable'. The fluidity and ambiguity of borders also lead observers to move away from the conventional concept of legal-territorial division and to characterize borders as complex assemblages (Sohn 2016) or multi-scalar entities (Laine 2016).

The multi-scalar nature of state borders is fully reflected in China, especially with the special status of Hong Kong and Macao. In these two cities, borders exist not only internally but also right in the middle of central growth hubs instead of at the periphery. Under the 'One Country, Two Systems' principle, Hong Kong was established as a Special Administrative Region when it returned to China in 1997 after some 150 years of British rule. Two years later, in 1999, the Macao Special Administrative Region was set up, ending more than 400 years of Portuguese rule. Under the Sino-British and Sino-Portuguese Joint Declarations and the Basic Laws of the two regions, Hong Kong and Macao are allowed to preserve their capitalist market system and to retain their status as independent customs zones.

The establishment of the two regions amounts to what Ong (2004) calls zoning technologies in forging a kind of creative exceptionalism. They are zones of political exception to communist rule, created to accommodate islands of distinct governing regimes within the broader landscape of normalized rule. The two Special Administrative Regions thus possess their own mini-constitution, political institutions, legal framework, and law enforcement system, which in effect sustain a form of sovereignty under one China that is variegated but linked. To uphold these two zones of exception, borders between mainland China and the two Special Administrative Regions are maintained, within a broader unified national border. As a result, the flow of goods, finance, and people across the sub-borders are controlled and regulated by local state authorities, in much the same way as at national borders. Smart and Smart (2008: 192) astutely point out the anomalous nature of the border regime in Hong Kong: on the one hand, Hong Kong has one of the most open borders to the world; on the other hand, Hong Kong also keeps an exclusive border to separate the territory from its own sovereign country. Such an ambiguous border regime provides ample opportunities for shadow exchange. The historical role of Hong Kong and Macao as entrepot centres for shadow trade not only revived but also further strengthened after their return to China. Their pivotal links in the global value chains will be explored in detail shortly.

Similar ambiguity can also be found in Kinmen and Matsu, the two coastal islands off Fujian province under the control of the Taiwan government. Under wartime arrangements, communication between mainland China and Taiwan had to go through a third destination such as Hong Kong and Macao. The wartime military administration was subsequently lifted in 1992. Since then, the two islands have served as a buffer zone between mainland China and Taiwan under the so-called mini-three-links policy, where direct trade, transportation, and postal services between mainland China and the two islands are allowed. Once sparsely populated and peripheral, Kinmen and Matsu have become central hubs for shadow exchange, linking Taiwan to China under the new policy.

Shadow Power

Under porous borders, the expansion of shadow exchange on a global scale has major implications for the international political economy. It affects the transnational flow of resources and global value chains, hence changing the course of economic globalization. It further alters the pattern of transnational connectivity and the regional division of labour, which in turn may redefine the power configuration in the global order. While the extent of these changes is still unfolding, their consequences cannot be underestimated.

Observers have raised the question about how the configuration will look if shadow networks are charted onto the world map (Hall 2012). As Nordstrom (2011:13) puts it: 'Would the whirls and eddies marking the centers of economic gravity in the world – and the attendant political power – produce a far different constellation of identities, nations and regions than that familiar from textbooks?' Nordstrom has some doubts about the possibility of such exercise because of the opacity of global shadow exchange. In her view, since no exact data exists on any gross shadow domestic product, shadow multinationals, or shadow trade volumes, no one can say who the superpowers of the extra-legal world might be.

This doubt is, however, largely overstated. There is no shortage of documentation about some of the hubs in the global shadow economy. For years, Columbia has been the notorious home of global drug cartels. This is followed by Mexico, where drug cartels have gradually expanded southward into neighbouring Guatemala in recent years. The Tri-Border Area of South America has also emerged as the new centre of transnational crime, alongside places such as Dubai, Turkey, and Moldova (Gilman et al. 2013). Ukraine was once seen as another 'epicenter of global badness', which provided one-stop shopping for possibly anything (Keefe 2013). In Asia, the Golden Triangle has long been the largest supplier of opium until it was superseded by Afghanistan and Myanmar. Bangkok is a regional hub for human traffickers, weapon smugglers, and document forgers. Not surprisingly, many illicit hubs are located in major cities of relatively coherent states with good transportation infrastructures (Patrick 2011).

As for the mass smuggling activities that concern us here, the pattern is no less observable. Many transnational shadow value chains in fact involve stable, trackable routes and networks radiating from certain nodal centres. One of which, without doubt, is China. With its large number of land and maritime borders, as well as various zones of exceptions, China has positioned itself like a spider at the centre of a giant transnational web, facilitated by the Belt and Road Initiative which extends its connecting reach across various continents.

Furthermore, in tandem with China's growing dominance in the global value chains is its increasing leverage in the shadow value chain. That is why we speak of the shadow power of China. It is the capacity to influence other nations and overseas communities through leveraging economic advantages for their benefit via various forms of shadow exchange. Such power derives from China's position as a key supplier and consumer of shadow products, as a transit hub, and as a nodal centre for worldwide shadow networks. More importantly, global China's transnational shadow exchange relies on a range of informal arrangements and practices, including modes of governance, networks, agential actors, rules of transaction, and border-crossing politics that are not predicated upon formal institutions or targeted at the open economy. These hidden dimensions constitute the governing logics of this obscure process and are the artifices of shadow power. They are the next subjects of our analysis.

3 The Nodal Shadow Centre

Global shadow exchanges are concentrated in a few nodal centres, and the most prominent one is undoubtedly China. China assumes several simultaneous roles: as a manufacturing centre of low-cost products, counterfeit items, and knockoffs; as a consumption centre for smuggled products; as a distribution centre or entrepot for products transacted through informal channels; and as a financial centre for shadow banking and money laundering. Over the years, China has become an international sourcing centre, a clearing house, and a meeting point for smuggling networks across the world.

Internally, there is a division of labour among various Chinese cities. Some cities serve as supplier centres and trading enclaves for shadow exports. Some function as nationwide distribution centres through which goods are smuggled into China and shuttled across the country. And a handful of cities have become the intermediary centres for shadow finance and money laundering. Together they form a complete chain of shadow operation from production, supply, distribution, import, and export to financing. The discussion in the following section tracks the flow of shadow goods and services in and out of China through these cities and underlines China's nodal position in the shadow world.

The World's Factory and Its Illicit Industries

From the outset, China's role as a shadow trading centre has developed in conjunction with its rise as a world factory. A quick glance at some statistics shows that this rise is spectacular by every measure. On the eve of China's market reform, its share of global trade stood at less than 1 per cent. By the end of the 1990s, Chinese goods of all kinds had reached every corner of the earth. By 2020, China became the top exporting country with nearly 15 per cent of the share in global trade, followed by the United States (8 per cent), Germany (7.8 per cent), the Netherlands (3.8 per cent), and Japan (3.6 per cent). China was the largest export destination for thirty-three countries and the largest source of imports for sixty-five countries. An UNCTAD report rightly describes China as a 'trade titan' (Nicita and Razo 2021). Even more impressive is China's manufacturing capacity. China contributed to almost 30 per cent of the global manufacturing output in 2019, nearly double that of the United States (17 per cent), and vastly exceeding Japan (7.5 per cent) and Germany (5.3 per cent). Even during the Covid-19 pandemic, China maintained its dominant position, prompting *The Economist* (23 June 2020) to conclude that China is the world's factory more than ever.

Stunning as these figures may be, this is however only part of the story. Another part concerns shadow activities, which are not yet accounted for. Take the growing trade in counterfeit goods for example. China has contributed to an overwhelming proportion in this expansion. The United States Chamber of Commerce (2016: 3) estimated that China was the source of more than 72 per cent of global trade-related counterfeiting between 2010 and 2014, amounting to more than USD285 billion. Hong Kong accounted for another 14 per cent. Counterfeit goods amounted to an equivalent of 12.5 per cent of goods exported by China, accounting for more than 1.5 per cent of its GDP. In brief, China and Hong Kong contributed to a total of 86 per cent of global physical counterfeiting, totalling USD396.5 billion each year in the 2010s.

In value terms, the biggest shares of Chinese counterfeit goods were footwear, clothing, leather goods, electrical equipment, watches, medical equipment, perfumes, toys, jewellery, and pharmaceuticals (OECD/EUIPO 2016). In fact, Teo and Yoon (2019: 3) observe that for every legitimate industry in China, there is an illicit counterpart, both in physical goods production and service provision. There are clones and knockoffs that range from foodstuffs, luxury consumables, pharmaceuticals, and computer software to taxi services, Apple Stores, and missile components. Some go so far as to fake an entire corporation and its products. Computer manufacturer NEC was shocked to discover a computer model that it had never made, but yet marketed under its brand name. A Chinese factory had developed a whole range of products, manufacturing capacities, and distribution networks. Some factories and workers genuinely believed that they were working for NEC, as did some business partners (Teo and Yoon 2019: 4). In essence, one cannot avoid the shadow economy in China. Even the 2010 Shanghai World Expo – the largest World Expo to date – could not escape shadow operations. It was estimated that of the CNY350 billion (USD45 billion) spent in the preparation for the Expo, at least CNY800 million (USD100 million) came from shadow finance (Tomisaka 2010).

Many factors lead to the proliferation of illicit industries, both on the supply and demand sides. First and foremost is the ease of market entry for manufacturers. This in turn relates to weak licencing and intellectual property rights protection. On top of this, illicit industries have benefited from a general reluctance of local state authorities to eradicate them since they contribute substantially to local employment and economic growth. Worse still, some of these factories are actually township and village enterprises owned by the local authorities. Furthermore, the current consumption culture creates a huge demand for copies and knockoffs because the genuine products are far too pricey for ordinary consumers. Most people prefer to pay less for a product that highly resembles the original, albeit of lesser quality.

As a matter of fact, the low production cost in China is partly attributable to its shadow economy. On the one hand, wages have been kept low because of the supply of a large number of migrant workers and informal labourers. At the same time, the costs of living have also been low because of the availability of shadow products for daily needs. The then Premier Li Keqiang stirred up a heated debate in 2020 when he mentioned in a press conference that more than 600 million people in China (i.e. nearly half of the entire population) were earning CNY1000 (USD130) a month on average. One can imagine that these people rely extensively on shadow products and services for their subsistence. For them, the shadow economy is their lifeblood.

In the same vein, shadow banking has been the lifeblood of many small and medium-sized enterprises. Despite their profit-earning ability, these enterprises have difficulty obtaining bank loans and credit from state-owned banks. The latter prefer to lend to state-owned enterprises partly under the pressure of local governments and partly to reduce credit risk. Consequently, small enterprises can only resort to shadow banking (Tsai 2002). This includes not only informal financial networks, such as rotating credit associations, private consortia, and crowdfunding, but also shadow finance disguised under the operation of formal entities in the name of pawnshops and consignment shops (Ngo 2018). The nationwide shadow finance networks also serve as a convenient gateway to move money in and out of China to escape remittance control and to launder money. The size of shadow finance in China is staggering. An official study has estimated the size of shadow banking to be as high as 31 per cent of China's GDP in 2010, 38 per cent in 2011, and 53 per cent in 2012 (Yan and Li 2014: 62).

As expected, widespread corruption also contributes significantly to the proliferation of shadow activities. For a long period of time, bribery has been a common way of getting things done, be it cadre promotion, state licencing, rent seeking, obtaining preferential treatment, buying regulatory convenience, or strengthening political and business connections (Gong 2006; Ngo 2008; Wedeman 2022). Corruption not only protects shadow operations from official crackdowns but also grows an underground market for luxury and counterfeit goods where officials can redeem luxury gifts and obtain cash in return. Subsequently, this underground market becomes part and parcel of the bureaucratic culture that features the exchange of gifts between officials and even between governmental units.

Finally, the mixing of legitimate, licenced components and services with illicit production and distribution makes it hard to detect shadow operations. The problematic dichotomy of the formal–informal can be seen here. Some well-established multinationals are known to use informal labour and shadow components in their production. The global electronic manufacturing services leader Foxconn offers a notorious example of using informal workers in their factories in China. The once-highly respected multi-billion investment company Tomorrow Holding was recently indicted for engaging in shadow finance and money laundering. The Taiwanese producer of anti-tactical ballistic missiles was found to use fake components sourced from the Chinese online shopping platform Taobao.

These factors together account for the proliferation of illicit activities originating from China. What deserves further attention is the expansion of such activities beyond the Chinese border. Under the heightened economic drive, not only have Chinese manufactures gone global, but illicit industries have also expanded from traditional, territorially based personal networks to rational, deterritorialized, non-kinship-based organizations on a global scale (Teo and Yoon 2019: 12). This expansion is facilitated by state policies, albeit unintentionally. In 2013, the Chinese government launched a plan under the so-called Silk Road Economic Belt and the Twenty-First Century Maritime Silk Road. Often abbreviated to the Belt and Road Initiative, this grand strategy comprises massive land- and sea-based developmental plans, including roads, railways, ports, energy pipelines, and telecommunications projects, that link China to Western Europe via Central Asian states, Iran, Turkey, Russia, the Caucasus, and the Balkans. The maritime routes connect China to South Asia, Southeast Asia, the Middle East, Africa, and Europe through seaports via the South China Sea, the Indian Ocean, the Red Sea, and the Mediterranean Sea.

The Initiative is intended to be a long-term, cross-continental, grand strategy for fostering a new geo-economic order that embraces development and connectivity. Notwithstanding this, the aggressive implementation of the Initiative has given additional impetus to the shadow trade between participating countries. From the outset, there has been a significant overlap between Belt and Road routes and trafficking routes (Kupatadze and Kumar 2022). Furthermore, the improved connectivity has vastly facilitated transnational shadow exchanges, since the development of infrastructural linkages and logistical corridors has benefited both legal and illegal trade activities (Ngo and Hung 2020). As will be discussed in the next section, a large number of traders and smugglers from Belt and Road countries have flocked into China in the guise of joining the Initiative (Wong 2021). Trading activities and the deliberate mixing of both licit and illicit exchanges have multiplied. In addition, border cities that were once perceived as peripheral regions have taken on new roles and meanings. Places such as Huoerguosi–Khorgos, Suifenhe–Pogranichny/Ussuriysk, Ruili–Muse, and Dongxing–Móng Cái are now seen as the intersections of civilizations. They are meant to be forefronts of the Belt and Road Initiative and gateways of resource flow. Without exception, all such border towns have become centres of shadow exchanges. Border communities have wasted little time in taking advantage of the Belt and Road policies to expand their shadow activities. This reminds us of Strange's (1996: 111–112) insight that a new phase in the international political economy emerges when illicit groups expand their activities outside their home territories in as much the same way as the multinationals, enabling the once-discrete, national illegal markets to join together to form a single world market.

Supplier Centres and Export Outlets

Since the 1990s, a number of Chinese cities have emerged as supplier centres and trading enclaves for ordinary as well as shadow products heading for Asia, Eurasia, Africa, and the Middle East. Their role has been further consolidated under the Belt and Road Initiative. These nodal hubs of shadow exchange include Yiwu, Guangzhou, Beijing, Ruili, Dongxing, Huoerguosi, and Suifenhe. In the past, aside from Beijing and Guangzhou, the other cities named did not belong to the class of top-tier urban metropolises such as Shanghai, Shenzhen, Hangzhou, Chengdu, Nanjing, or Tianjin – all focal points of national industrial and commercial development. Yet they are now unmatched in their importance as intersections of global shadow networks.

The most extensive shadow networks can be traced to Yiwu in Zhejiang province, a small county-level city that was once unknown even to most Chinese. Before the Covid-19 outbreak, Yiwu was home to the largest commodity market in the world. It was included in the Notorious Markets List published by the United States Trade Representative (2011), which describes Yiwu as 'a center for wholesaling of infringing goods' and 'the origin of many counterfeit goods available internationally'. Goods sourced in Yiwu are exported to more than 200 countries, including those in the EU and ASEAN, as well as top importers such as Iran, India, Egypt, UAE, Saudi Arabia, Brazil, Iraq, and Algeria. On the eve of the pandemic, some 1,500 containers left the city each day.

Yiwu has become a pilgrim centre for foreign traders, especially from developing countries. The large international community which has emerged consists of both sojourners and visitors from a broad array of countries and regions, including most notably India, Korea, Iran, Iraq, Pakistan, Afghanistan, Russia, Central Asia, and various nations of Africa and Latin America (Jacobs, 2016: 80). One study estimates that some 14,000 foreign traders were residing in Yiwu before the Covid-19 outbreak (Ibañez-Tirado and Marsden 2020: 139). These were sojourners with renewable one- or two-year visas. Thousands of trading or cargo companies have been set up in Yiwu to procure local manufactures for export to their home country. The sojourners also provide sourcing services to no fewer than 200,000 itinerant traders from the Middle East and North Africa who visit Yiwu regularly to look for profitable merchandise (Belguidoum and Pleiz 2015). In essence, Yiwu functions as the meeting point for different trading networks (Harper and Amrith 2012).

Among these trading networks is a prominent group of Afghan traders. A recent study (Ibañez-Tirado and Marsden 2020: 145) counted 182 trading offices registered to Afghans in Yiwu, procuring merchandise to Afghanistan, Pakistan, and Tajikistan. In particular, they play a key role in smuggling Chinese merchandise from Afghanistan to Pakistan after goods arrive in Afghanistan. Afghan traders are also active in exporting Chinese products to the Arabian Peninsula, especially to Dubai, Saudi Arabia, and Oman (Marsden 2018). Some also engage in the trade between China, Russia, and Ukraine.

Another prominent group in Yiwu comprises Central Asian traders. Compared to Afghan traders, the number of traders from Tajikistan and Uzbekistan is relatively smaller. Ibañez-Tirado and Marsden (2020: 142) recorded three well-established trading and cargo companies and two restaurants from Tajikistan, and fifteen trading and cargo companies from Uzbekistan. The rest of the Central Asian traders are temporary visitors who come for short business trips, buying goods in Yiwu and moving them to Tajikistan, Uzbekistan, Russia, and even to Germany and the United States. Part of this trading path involves shadow operations. One example is the smuggling of toys and leggings, which are subject to import tariffs in Uzbekistan. Traders will source their leggings from Yiwu, import them to Tajikistan, and then smuggle them across the border to Uzbekistan. After arrival, the goods are labelled 'Made in Uzbekistan' and sold under a local brand (Ibañez-Tirado and Marsden 2020: 144).

Trading activities in Yiwu are concentrated in several markets. The Futian Market, which hosts more than 70,000 shops, is the main wholesale market for daily commodities such as stationery, toys, souvenirs, cosmetics, jewellery, accessories, and household goods. Others such as the Huangyuan Garment Market – which sells jeans, sportwear, and garments of all types – and the Yiwu Furniture Market are also popular among foreign traders. In addition to trade in local manufactures, transactions include the wholesale acquisition of counterfeit products, pirated goods, and knockoffs. There are numerous local companies that accept orders to produce fake labels, boxes, and packages for fabricated goods (Ibañez-Tirado and Marsden 2020: 141).

Yiwu's neighbouring county-level city Keqiao is less famous but equally popular. It was a trading hub for textiles and fabrics of all kinds during the 2010s. No fewer than 10,000 Indian traders were based in Keqiao, making it the largest Indian community in China and earning the name Little India (Cheuk 2016). Furthermore, Islamic quarters and Arab quarters with shops and restaurants run by the sojourners abound in Yiwu to cater for the needs of different trading communities.

Following Yiwu, Guangzhou is another supplier centre. Before the pandemic, Guangzhou was home to a vast community of African sojourners, traders, translators, and brokers (Bredeloup 2012; Gilles 2015). The exact number of Africans residing in Guangzhou remains debatable. Official figures claimed that around 16,000–20,000 Africans legally resided in the mid-2010s. However, since a high percentage of African migrants are undocumented, semi-official and unofficial sources estimate that as many as 200,000–500,000 Africans were living in Guangzhou during the period. In addition, a large number of short-term African visitors can be found at any time. These are traders who come to purchase goods and place production orders. In 2015, more than 580,000 entries were recorded at the airport and land borders (Haugen 2019a: 301). A 2019 report finds that among the inbound visitors who stayed more than four days in China, African visitors made up the largest proportion (World Tourism Alliance 2019).

Most Africans in Guangzhou come from Nigeria and the sub-Sahara region. They outnumber other groups such as Arabs, Argentines, Filipinos, Turks, and Americans. Their main areas of activities are located in Xiaobei and Sanyuanli. Many Nigerians reside in the neighbouring Foshan city. Enclaves of African traders can be found in multi-storey emporiums offering a wide range of services such as visa application, packaging, shipping arrangement, transportation, restaurants, cafes, and medical services (Jin et al. 2021: 5). Cottage industries flourished to meet the needs of African traders, such as bazaars, hotels, restaurants, money exchange, shipping agencies, and translators (Neuwirth 2012: 73–74).

Notwithstanding the shadow nature of many of such trading activities per se, the presence of the African traders is in itself a shadow phenomenon. Many Africans overstay in Guangzhou illegally, and work or conduct business without a licence or registration (Neuwirth 2012: 72–73). Under the strict visa policy and residential registration regime in China, many traders use student visas and purport to be African students. Others go underground and hide in neighbouring villages. In fact, they change their legal status several times during their stay – first entering China with a valid visa using falsified documents, then becoming undocumented migrants when they overstay, and then regaining a legal status if they manage to get a residence permit through the backdoor (Haugen 2012, 2019b).

These traders source low-priced products and counterfeit goods in China, and supply them to the African diaspora in different parts of the world (including Europe and the United States) and to their home countries. They have come up with innovative ways of moving goods to Africa by mixing formal channels (such as container shipments, groupage, air cargo, and courier service) with informal arrangements (such as suitcase couriering and buying luggage allowances via logistic brokers) (Haugen 2019a).

Besides Africans, Kyrgyz traders and middlemen are also active in Guangzhou. They organize buying trips for their Russian-speaking clientele (from Central Asia to the Caucasus) and coordinate meetings with local manufacturers, serving as translators during business talks and handling cargo shipments as well as undertaking quality checks on behalf of their clientele. Many of them speak Putonghua. Schröder (2020: 130) describes the role of these Kyrgyz middlemen in Guangzhou as 'globalization from the middle', brokering and mediating between informal and formal aspects of the regional value chain.

A similar situation is found in another supplier centre – Beijing. The Yabaolu Market used to be a sourcing outpost for Russian-speaking buyers, attracting traders from Russia, the Baltic states, the Caucasus, Ukraine, Eastern Europe, and Central Asia. Nicknamed Russia Town, it is one of the largest garment markets in China. Besides clothing, shoes, accessories, counterfeit handbags, and knockoffs, other merchandise such as electronic and digital products and kitchenware can also be found. Supporting businesses – such as cargo services, banks, warehouses, travel agencies, restaurants, and even hairdressers – proliferate in the neighbourhood (Fehlings 2020: 97). Russian is widely spoken in the area, even by many Chinese shopkeepers, making it a truly Russian enclave.

All in all, a nationwide shadow merchandise market/sector has developed in China, with locational specialization in different products catering for particular groups of international traders and trade destinations. The market is supported by all kinds of auxiliary services from lodging, translation, logistics, and brokerage to the fabrication of fake labels and falsified permits. It is a dynamic market that defies the open-shadow boundaries. Here formal and informal transactions of both licit and illicit products are mixed comfortably in daily life.

Entrepots and Transit Points

Besides supplier centres, there are numerous entrepots and transit points for shadow exports/re-exports in China. Most of them are located in the border regions, which were once peripheral areas with long histories of cross-border exchange, but have been revived by the Belt and Road Initiative to become central hubs for shadow trading. In fact, many border economic cooperation zones and border trade zones were established at the border towns well before the promulgation of the Belt and Road Initiative (Hu and Yu 2020). These border zones allow tariff-free trade between border residents for commodities below a certain value and quantity – creating a grey area for crowd smuggling, by allowing traders to split up trading commodities into permissible quantities. The benefits of border zones are brought to light under the Belt and Road Initiative, as seen by the substantial volume of transnational trade diverted to these zones to escape taxation. This has led to a rejuvenation in the long-existing cultural ties between the border communities.

One eye-catching example is Huoerguosi in Xinjiang, bordering Khorgos in Kazakhstan. Kazakhstan is an active player in the Belt and Road Initiative, striving to diversify its economy beyond energy exports (Bitabarova 2018). Within a few years, the once-peripheral town of Huoerguosi has become an epicentre of the Eurasian trade, thanks to the state-led strategy to 'centralize the periphery' (Alff 2016a: 369). Under the Belt and Road Initiative, all outbound trains from China to Europe stop at Huoerguosi for transshipment. By 2014, cargo passing through Huoerguosi accounted for half of Xinjiang's import/export volume (Hong Kong Trade Development Council 2016). Three years later, bilateral trade between China and Kazakhstan surged by 40 per cent to reach USD18 billion in 2017 (*Pengbai Xinwen* 25 July 2018). Shortly before the Covid-19 outbreak, a total of 34.8 million metric tons of goods passed through Huoerguosi in 2018, ranking it the top among a total of seventy-seven border road ports in China (*Annual Report of China Ports* 2019).

Besides being a trading hub in Eurasia, Huoerguosi is also an epicentre of shadow exchanges. Most of these shadow activities take place within its border zone – at the Huoerguosi–Khorgos International Centre for Boundary Cooperation (hereafter Khorgos International Centre). Formally opened in 2012, this trans-border free trade zone consists of two parts: an area of 3.43 km^2 is located in Chinese territory, while the other 1.85 km^2 lies on Kazakh soil. The Centre is supposed to be a bonded zone for duty-free shoppers from both the Chinese and Kazakh sides. It is designed as a visa-free zone where citizens of the two countries can trade and shop. Since Kazakhstan is a member of the Eurasian Economic Union, goods that pass through Khorgos can be distributed freely throughout the Union without any additional customs inspections or duties. This includes goods bought in the Khorgos International Centre, because of which the Centre serves as a convenient gateway for Chinese products to enter the Eurasian market (Figure 1). According to Chinese official statistics, 91,100 metric tons of Chinese goods transited through the Khorgos International Centre in 2017 (*Annual Report of China Ports* 2018). Based on the daily volume of untaxed goods that passed through the Kazakh border checkpoints, it is estimated that no less than 50,000 metric tons of goods were

Figure 1 Goods inside the Khorgos International Centre.

smuggled to Kazakhstan during the same period through shadow trade (Fieldwork in Khorgos 2018). In other words, more than half of the trade volume in the Khorgos International Centre was exchanged through illicit means. The sizable trade volume makes it impossible to use conventional suitcase trading as a means of smuggling. Smuggling is therefore carried out through specific mechanisms.

Most of the goods available in the Khorgos International Centre originate from Yiwu, Guangzhou, and other supplier centres. In essence, the Centre serves as a transit point and wholesale outlet for Chinese products. It is here that these products are shuttled through border control via shadow channels (Figure 2). They are reassembled in Almaty and other neighbouring cities, to be further distributed to the rest of Central Asia, Middle East, Europe, and Russia. Such an operation is typical in most other border cities. For instance, at the Suifenhe border in Heilongjiang, border-crossing activities are dominated by underground syndicates moving goods to Pogranichy and Ussuriysk (Fieldwork in Suifenhe and Ussuriysk 2019). The border town of Heihe performs the same transit function for Chinese goods going to Blagoveshchensk – the home of a large Chinese expatriate community that organizes distribution networks for the Siberian region (Fieldwork in Heihe and Blagoveshchensk 2019). It is believed that most of the textile products in Chita, Blagoveshchensk, and

Figure 2 Crowd smuggling in Khorgos.

Khabarovsk are imported from China through shuttle trade or smuggling (Fedorova 2012: 115).

In southwestern China, similar transit centres exist in Dongxing (Guangxi) and Ruili (Yunnan). Dongxing is a county-level city bordering the Vietnamese city of Móng Cái. More than two-thirds of its 150,000 inhabitants were transient migrants engaged mostly in border trade with Vietnam before China implemented a lockdown during the pandemic. Textile products from Yiwu are smuggled through Dongxing into Vietnam, where they are labelled 'Made in Vietnam' before being re-exported to the United States (Fieldwork in Dongxing and Móng Cái 2019). Ruili is another peripheral town that has turned into a major transit centre. With a population of merely 210,000, it once registered an annual passenger traffic of nearly eighteen million, the largest volume of passenger traffic after Macao and Hong Kong before the pandemic (*Annual Report of China Ports* 2018). It shares a 170-km border with Myanmar and was host to more than 50,000 Burmese who came as workers, students, and traders before the Covid-19 lockdown. A large number of them engaged in open as well as shadow trade in jade, animal parts, consumables, and electronic products (Møller 2021).

In addition to these transit points, several cities, including Hong Kong and Macao, have emerged as shadow entrepots for re-exports. An exemplary case is

Shishi, a small county-level coastal city in Fujian province. Shishi is notorious for smuggling activities and counterfeit produce. According to Byrne et al. (2021), Shishi has been a base for fuel smuggling for decades. Intriguingly, the supply comes from Taiwan, because of government subsidies and tax exemptions. The Taiwanese government has offered a 14 per cent fuel subsidy for fishing vessels since 2008, before reducing it to 5 per cent in 2021. Domestic fishing vessels are exempted from commodity and business taxes on diesel and marine fuel oil, as well as from business taxes on gasoline. In addition, duty-free diesel is also made available for foreign tankers that use the seaports in Taiwan. As a result, it was reported in 2018 that the diesel price in mainland China was about 43 per cent higher than that in Taiwan (Byrne et al. 2021: 11). Fuel smuggling into China has therefore become a very lucrative business, with the Chinese army playing a key role in the business, to the extent of eroding the market share held by the monopolistic Sinopec and PetroChina by over 30 per cent (Byrne et al. 2021: 12). In general, smugglers use foreign-flagged oil tankers or fishing vessels to load fuel from a Taiwanese port. Some then head to Fujian; others would sail towards North Korea. At specific offshore locations, they transfer the oil to either feeds or delivery vessels to be delivered to the destination. Byrne et al. (2021: 23) found that at least thirteen foreign-flagged tankers have been delivering fuel to North Korea since 2019. Most of the vessels are owned by companies registered in Hong Kong with only a mail address and no demonstrable business profile.

The Shishi smuggling network was once spearheaded by Lai Changxing of the Yuanhua Group, who built a multibillion-dollar empire that smuggled oil, cigarettes, automobiles, and electronics into China. When the smuggling ring was brought to light, more than 700 state officials were charged for their connection to Yuanhua (Wank 2009: 83). Based in Shishi, Lai's network was found to be embedded in Fujianese gangs active in the North Point district, which is home to the biggest Fujianese community in Hong Kong. Lai was succeeded by several smugglers who are alleged to have established an illicit fuel supply chain to North Korea. They are all based in Shishi, which has emerged as the critical hub in North Korea's supply chain as well as the connecting node between China and Southeast Asia in shadow exchanges involving cigarettes, drugs, fuel, wildlife, ivory, timber, and counterfeit goods (Byrne et al. 2021).

Special Zones for Shadow Exchange

Border zones such as the Khorgos International Centre are in essence grey areas deliberately created by the state to take advantage of their plasticity and informal connectivity. In this regard, nowhere is their role more prominent than that in Hong Kong, Macao, Kinmen, and Matsu. They are the nodal centres within the central hub, and serve as the shadow entrepots for a large volume of goods going in and out of China. Unlike other border towns in China, their separate customs status sets them apart from other transit points. Such a unique geopolitical position has turned them into irreplaceable entrepots for the massive resource flow of people, money, and goods. Despite some half-hearted attempts by the local governments to curb excessive smuggling activities, cross-border shadow exchanges continue to flourish, even during the pandemic when border crossings were highly controlled.

Earlier in Section 2, we discussed the presence of securitized sub-borders between mainland China and the two Special Administrative Regions of Hong Kong and Macao. With the passage of time, these sub-borders have become porous (Smart and Lin 2004). This happens as the economies on both sides of the borders become increasingly integrated, with people who cross borders behaving more like commuters in a large metropolitan area. An increasing number of people now work, live, shop, and attend schools on both sides of the border. In the 2010s, an annual average of more than forty-five million and thirty million mainland visitors visited Hong Kong and Macao, respectively. A constant stream of people passes through the various checkpoints all year round. This volume of visitors is remarkable especially for Macao, whose population is less than 680,000. Given the vast number of visitors and daily commuters, border checks are at best nominal. The minimal checking arrangements and the crowded situation at border controls provide an enormous advantage for smugglers and suitcase traders who cross the borders every day.

Taking advantage of the open-trade policy in Hong Kong and Macao, traders import goods in any quantity into the two regions, and then smuggle them across the sub-borders to escape tariffs in mainland China. These products are commonly known as 'parallel goods'. They are not counterfeits or knockoffs but genuine products with reputable brand names. They are imported into Hong Kong and Macao legally, but 're-exported' to mainland China through informal channels. They are much cheaper than the same products imported directly into China, and are therefore in high demand by mainland consumers. Besides price considerations, product quality is another reason for the demand in parallel goods. Although China is a manufacturing centre of counterfeits and low-priced products, the dubious quality of products and services has damaged consumer confidence. Scandals involving food and consumption products abound: gutter oil, poisonous drinks, plastic eggs, zombie meat, contaminated cosmetics, counterfeit medicines, carcinogenic shampoo, and so on (Si et al. 2018; Sugita 2019). One extreme case occurred in 2008 when milk and infant formula were adulterated with toxic melamine, resulting in some 300,000 babies being affected and 54,000 of them hospitalized. One fallout from such scandals is that foreign imported brands are considered to be authentic and safe. Ironically, while many of the Chinese counterfeit and fake products are in high demand in developing countries, Chinese consumers choose to buy goods delivered via the shadow trade to avoid their own shadow products.

By virtue of being a free port, Hong Kong and Macao therefore serve as the main entrepots for foreign products into China. These range from luxury consumables, cosmetics, mobile phones to infant milk powder, instant noodles, baby napkins, and even frozen meat. They are delivered not only by organized syndicates but also by freelance couriers who commute daily across the sub-borders for study, work, and leisure. In one instance, amber from Ukraine and Russia was first shipped to Hong Kong and then carried by suitcase couriers to Shenzhen. Raw amber was then processed in Shenzhen and sold in Beijing and other cities. When the operation was busted, six tons of amber were uncovered (*Ming Pao* 28 October 2016). There are also reports of many amazing and innovative operations. For example, smugglers used drones to carry cables across the Shenzhen River. The 200-metre cable was fixed at one end in Shenzhen and at the other end in Hong Kong. Mobile phones put in a small canvas bag were then transported on this zip line from Hong Kong to Shenzhen. Some 10,000–15,000 mobile phones were transported each day, typically from midnight until dawn. A similar set-up used a cross-border tunnel instead of a zip line. Smugglers constructed a 600-metre-long pipeline, 6 metres beneath the ground across the riverbank of Shenzhen River, connecting Luofang village in Shenzhen and Lee Uk village in Hong Kong. Mobile phones and electronic parts were put in bags and pulled to the other end on the mainland (*Apple Daily* 30 March 2018).

Similar activities can be found in Kinmen and Matsu, the two outer islands under Taiwan's rule. When Sino-Australian relations worsened in 2020, trade sanctions were placed on Australian exports, including wheat, wine, beef, cotton, and lobsters. China's import of live Australian lobsters dropped from an annual volume of 8,400 metric tons to zero. However, within a short period of time, lobsters found their way to China through Kinmen and Matsu: no fewer than 3,000 Brolos lobsters on daily flights from Perth, Sydney, or Brisbane to Taiwan island and then onward to Kinmen and Matsu. Up to this point the lobsters remain legal imports. From there the lobsters are shipped to the open sea where mainland Chinese dealers receive the illegal lobster shipments. In 2022 alone, more than 2,300 metric tons of Australian lobsters were smuggled into China through this route. To ensure that lobsters are alive and fresh, a well-organized logistics chain is put in place to avoid any delays during transportation and customs clearance.

Lobsters are delivered to radar blind spots in the open sea to escape the attention of coastguards. Local residents speak of the existence of a 'smuggling association' in Kinmen and Matsu, which operates this sophisticated underground syndicate (*The Reporter* 9 January 2023).

Besides physical commodities, cross-border shadow exchanges also involve services. A police crackdown in 2016 unveiled the smuggling of human blood samples to Hong Kong for pregnancy and DNA tests, amounting to more than HKD230 million (USD30 million) worth of business. The syndicate collected over 50,000 blood samples from clients in more than thirty provinces and delivered them to a collecting point in Shenzhen. The samples were couriered by suitcase traders to Sheung Shui, Hong Kong. They were assembled in a medical clinic for repackaging and categorization, before being sent to various laboratories for specific tests. The test results were then sent back to mainland China (*Apple Daily* 4 July 2017).

Shadow Finance

The importance of shadow banking in financing small- and medium-sized enterprises in China has been shown earlier on. Shadow banking is also the major source of capital as well as investment outlet for illicit industries. Apart from these, there is one more dimension that underlines its significance: capital mobility. Similar to the situation when trade restrictions create the demand for the smuggling of physical commodities, illicit money transfer and laundering proliferate under state restrictions on capital flow. In China, the government maintains a closed capital account and restricts individuals and businesses from moving money across the Chinese border. Each individual can only remit an annual total of USD50,000 abroad, and can carry cash up to CNY20,000 (USD2,500) at each border crossing. Companies can exchange foreign currencies only upon approval, with proof of import invoices, and so on. This restriction creates a huge inconvenience even for normal businesses and lawful transactions. Furthermore, since the Chinese renminbi is not a freely convertible currency, there is a strong incentive for the rich to store their wealth elsewhere. In such circumstances, illicit money transfer comes to play a vital role. In addition to corrupt officials, legitimate businesses and ordinary people make use of the service to shuttle money in and out of China for the purposes of profit remittance, investment, pursuing studies abroad, and so on.

In this regard, Hong Kong and Macao serve not only as entrepots for goods but also as offshore havens for money, particularly before the high-handed crackdown in the early 2020s. By virtue of their free capital account regime, Hong Kong and Macao have the additional advantage of not taxing income that originates outside the territory. They therefore become the perfect destinations for parking and laundering money before the money is sent to other places such as the United States, Canada, and Australia. The Panama Papers exposé in 2016 confirmed that Hong Kong is the hub for Chinese enterprises, foreign investors, as well as the political elites to create offshore companies to bypass red tape, take advantage of tax breaks, and circumvent strict capital controls.

Shadow money transfer is usually done through the so-called hawala arrangement. It is a century-old system of long-distance financing that was widely practised in India, China, Southeast Asia, and the Middle East. It predates the modern banking system and played a central role in medieval trade along the silk roads, the Eastern Mediterranean, and the Indian Ocean. Although modern states have outlawed hawala by fiat, it remains much alive in some places to the very present day (El Qorchi et al. 2003). In a typical transaction, a mainland customer will give the money to a hawaladar based in mainland China, at an agreed exchange rate. Upon receiving the money, the hawaladar will ask his/her fellow operator in Hong Kong to pay the money back into specified bank accounts in Hong Kong. The transaction is done within a few minutes, without any money actually moving across the border.

In this shadow money chain, the southern city of Shenzhen serves as an intermediate transit point. Although underground capital markets are also active in other border regions, including Bohai, Guangxi, and Yunnan, as well as in Beijing and Shanghai, their size is much smaller than Shenzhen's. Most of the money is channelled into Shenzhen first, before being moved to Hong Kong. The reason is that it is difficult to avoid the formal banking system altogether, especially when huge sums of money are involved, which as a consequence allows transactions to be traced. In this way, anyone who wants to move CNY10 million (USD1.3 million) originally stored in a small city bank, say Mianyang in Sichuan, would easily be detectable because of the exceptionally large amount. In comparison, CNY10 million is a relatively small sum of money in cosmopolitan Shenzhen, so the transaction hardly invites any attention (Fieldwork in Hong Kong 2016).

An illustrative case about the popularity of hawala operations in China can be found in the underground financial network run by a businesswoman-cum-politician Du Ling. Du, who originated from the rural county Qingyuan in Guangdong province, established an underground financial empire based in Shenzhen and Hong Kong. She was prosecuted in 2007 for laundering more than CNY4.3 billion (USD550 million), with a daily transaction of more than CNY8 million (USD1 million). When Du's network was busted, it caused a rupture in the cash chain for China's offshore speculative capital, resulting in a stock market bump in Hong Kong (*Guangzhou Daily* 21 November 2007).

Compared to Hong Kong, Macao plays a smaller but not insignificant role in money laundering. This can be seen from another eye-opening case involving the Suncity Group – the top casino junket operator in Macao. Suncity is a listed company in the Hong Kong stock market, and covers businesses in tourism, film production, entertainment, catering, auction, resort hotel management, finance, and real estate development. Its VIP casino rooms once accounted for 45 per cent of all VIP room income in Macao. Although the VIP rooms operate legally under Macao law, they are well known for serving as informal bankers and hawaladars for capital fleeing mainland China (Varese 2015). Suncity established a vast network of agents in various provinces and cities in China, and provided one-stop services (transportation, hotel, loans, deposits, sex service, and so on) for customers who gambled in Macao (Lo and Kwok 2017). In 2021, Suncity's chairman and CEO, Alvin Chau, and twenty other high-level staff of Suncity were arrested and prosecuted for 289 crimes involving illegal gambling practices, offshore online gambling, underground finance, and money laundering (*Macau Daily* 2 September 2022). He was subsequently sentenced to eighteen years imprisonment. Shortly after Chau's arrest, another Macao casino junket operator, Levo Chan of the Tak Chun Group, was prosecuted for similar crimes.

The crackdown on Suncity and Tak Chun came as a big surprise in Macao because the role of the casino junkets in shadow finance has always been an open secret. Many believe that it was actually a decision from Beijing to stop capital flight. The crackdown led to the closure of most junket operations, causing a heavy blow to the Macao economy. It is worth noting that at its peak in the mid-2010s, the average annual casino income in Macao amounted to over MOP300 billion (USD38 billion), making Macao an enclave with one of the world's highest GDP per capita. The contribution of the shadow economy to Macao is beyond imagination.

All in all, China assumes multiple roles in global shadow exchange by virtue of being a world factory, supplier centre, transit hub, entrepot, as well as consumption haven of shadow goods and services. Yet this is only part of the story. An equally important part is the expansion of Chinese trading networks into different regions of the world and their connection to local shadow networks. The reach of such networks and the driving agents of this expansion have contributed to a new turn in globalization.

4 Networks and Agents

How do shadow networks operate? Who are recruited into the operation? These are important questions because they reveal the nature of mass shadow exchange when the participants include not only professional criminals but also ordinary people. These mass operations do not take place in a haphazard manner, even though individual participants seem to act independently. The vast majority of everyday smugglers, petty traders, and shadow brokers are in fact unwitting agents of organized syndicates, corporations, and even the state. Such operations are typically channelled through stable, trackable routes and networks radiating from a number of nodal centres, notably China. Many shadow brokers are either Chinese or local players linked to Chinese networks. The involvement of ordinary people and local groups allows Chinese networks to extend their tentacles far and wide.

Rhizomatic Networks

One of the contributing factors to the rising shadow power of China is its long-existing diasporic networks. It is estimated that more than thirty-three million Chinese migrants and their descendants reside in some 150 countries. This does not include the large number of sojourners and tourists. The widespread presence of Chinese communities enables diasporic ties to be easily mobilized for socio-economic purposes, including shadow exchange.

Studies on different regions have documented the intertwining connections among Chinese traders, diasporic settlers, sojourners, and local actors. These networks are rhizomatic in nature, reminding us of the idea suggested by Deleuze and Guattari (1988) that any point of contact in the network can be connected to another; an established network of exchanges may break up only to be reconnected along old or new lines. Smugglers in these networks exploit capillary-like routes that criss-cross formal and informal markets and commercial practices, moving goods and money across multiple boundaries (Ibañez-Tirado and Marsden 2020: 138).

Shadow traders prefer to work with members of their own ethnic group and/or diasporic group because of pragmatic considerations, such as ease of communication in the same language or dialect, proximity to work and residence, and the higher possibility of contract enforcement by means of extra-legal controls (Fehlings 2020: 103–104). This applies not only to Chinese traders but also other ethnic traders from Central Asia, Russia, Eurasia, and Africa.

Among the transnational networks, it is not uncommon to find diasporic Chinese traders controlling the upstream wholesale trade of shadow imports in host countries, although other diasporic groups also play a part in the rest of the chain. Given the transnational nature of shadow operations, no single ethnic group can organize the entire shadow value chain on its own. The linkage between transnational and local networks is vital since the latter provide the indigenous know-how for running shadow operations in the local settings.

Collaborations at different border crossings, transfer hubs, wholesale centres, and distribution outlets abound, particularly before the Covid-19 pandemic drastically impacted the situation on the ground. In the trans-Eurasian shadow trade, the brokering links between the ethnic minorities in China and their counterparts in Central Asia play an instrumental role (Laruelle and Peyrouse 2009; Alff 2017). These minority groups include, among others, the Dungans, the diasporic Uyghurs, the Kazakhs, and the Hui Chinese in Xinjiang. Dungan traders were among the first in Central Asia to establish reliable and long-standing business relations with China before and shortly after the Soviet break-up. The Dungans in Kazakhstan are Sinophone Muslims, most of whom are descendants of Chinese refugees originally from Shaanxi province. The Dungans in Kyrgyzstan, in contrast, are mainly from Gansu province. By taking advantage of their ethnolinguistic and religious lineages, these diasporic traders have successfully developed close business relations with partners in China as well as other diasporic groups in Southeast Asia. They travel regularly to Urumqi, Yiwu, and other trading hubs in China to source their supplies. Some sojourners have established their own networks alongside the Chinese ones. The Afghan network in Yiwu is a good example. Ethnicity plays an important role since traders share and exchange information about their compatriots' activities and the trustworthiness of their trading partners (Marsden 2016).

The buyers' networks in Beijing, Guangzhou, and Yiwu are closely linked to the wholesale networks in many trading hubs, including Dordoi (Bishkek, Kyrgyzstan), Kara-Suu (Osh, Kyrgyzstan), Sed'moi (Odessa, Ukraine), and Lilo Bazroba (Tbilisi, Georgia). During the 2000s, the Dordoi Bazaar served as a centre of exchanges between China, Kyrgyzstan, and Central Asia, with total transactions valued at several billion US dollars, providing more than 40,000 people with incomes (Alff 2016b: 441; Spector 2017). Likewise, Fehlings (2020: 97) observes that more than 40 per cent of the merchandise sold in Lilo Bazroba in 2017 came from China. Nearly 20 per cent of the respondents working in Lilo travel regularly or occasionally to China to source their goods. With the advancement in mobile technology, traders and sojourners in China can easily get in touch with their family and business partners in their home country, regularly exchanging views about what to buy or order. Chinese factories are usually very flexible and efficient. They respond quickly to buyers' demands and can adapt to product modifications within a short period of time after receiving orders. Meanwhile, Chinese traders have wasted little time in taking advantage of the Belt and Road Initiative to expand their informal trading networks into the Caucasus (Fehlings 2022).

In the trans-Siberian shadow trade, Chinese and Russian traders form a close network. Ussuriysk is one of the major transit hubs for smugglers in Russia.

Chinese goods are gathered in Ussuriysk before being distributed to the rest of Russia. In these shadow operations, the owners of smuggled goods are almost exclusively Chinese, who hire Russian couriers to shuttle goods across the border. More than 60 per cent of the local inhabitants of Pogranichny, the border town not far from Ussuriysk, are believed to be involved in the shadow trade (Fieldwork in Ussuriysk and Pogranichny 2019).

Some parallels can be found in Southeast Asia. For instance, the border town of Móng Cái is the major transit point for shadow imports from China. Goods such as Chinese textiles, stationery, and daily consumables are found in the Móng Cái bazaar for wholesale and retail (Figure 3). All the shop owners there are Chinese. Some of them commute daily across the border. Others hire Vietnamese shopkeepers to run the shops. A substantial portion of the imports is transported from Móng Cái to Hanoi and then redistributed to the rest of Vietnam (Fieldwork in Móng Cái 2019).

Obviously, not all shadow networks are run by Chinese. For instance, intricate smuggling networks are found along the trans-Saharan trade routes in Africa. Scheele (2012) highlights the flexibility of these ancient and long-existing networks in incorporating new routes, new kinship networks, and new political relationships. Yet even in these local networks, it is more often than not to find a Chinese connection. In West Africa, markets for apparel are dominated by low-cost Chinese imports. Chinese goods are often sent by sourcing agents in Yiwu and Guangzhou to Benin and Togo, and then re-exported to other West African markets through informal local networks (Benjamin et al. 2015). In Ghana, traders import more than a ton of jewellery

Figure 3 Parallel goods arrived at the Móng Cái bazaar.

from China each year (Haugen 2018). In Nigeria, Chinese shoes are in high demand although they are barred from entering Nigeria. They are usually imported first to Benin, where trade with China is unrestricted and customs duties low. Local shadow traders then carry the shoes across the border into Nigeria (Neuwirth 2012: 188). In Central Africa, a huge variety of Chinese and Asian textiles and garments are on sale, most of which are smuggled into Kinshasa (Democratic Republic of the Congo) via the border city of Brazzaville (Republic of the Congo). Kinshasa traders either travel to the migrant district of Poto-Poto in Brazzaville to source their products or place their orders by phone. The Brazzaville dealers, among them the Soninkes and Mourides, in turn import the products via their diasporic trading networks based in various trading hubs. The goods are then smuggled into Kinshasa through local syndicates (Ayimpam 2015).

Looking closely at these transnational networks, it can be seen that Chinese networks are present everywhere. They reach out like the giant web of a spider, ever expanding in size to maximize the catch. Moreover, they closely follow the routes of the official Belt and Road Initiative. This is no accident. The improvement in bilateral relationships between China and the participating countries under the Initiative has vastly enhanced transnational connectivity. Some traders have taken advantage of the improved connectivity to establish new footholds along the shadow silk roads; others who have been marginalized by state policies or are obliged to break up old networks go in search of new ones. As van Schendel (2020: 62) puts it, the Belt and Road projects have destroyed some shadow practices but reinforced others.

As much as traders have taken advantage of the shadow connectivity, the Chinese state has not been slow in capitalizing the political potential of the shadow networks. Leaders of diasporic shadow networks have been co-opted to serve as the eyes and ears of the Chinese state. In return they enjoy Beijing's blessings as prominent leaders of overseas Chinese communities and clanship associations, as well as the tacit toleration of the Chinese authorities towards their shadow operations in and out of China (*ProPublica* 12 July 2023).

Variety of Actors

In the shadow networks, a huge variety of actors can be found, including individuals, corporate actors, and institutional actors. Within each category, a plurality of players with vastly diverse backgrounds can be identified, some with astonishing origins. Many of them combine an ostensible role in the formal economy with an actual role in the shadow economy.

Individuals

Let us first look at some examples in the first category: individuals. From the outset, many studies of illicit trade have focused on petty traders. Typically, such petty traders are the inhabitants of frontier regions who take advantage of their proximity to the state border to shuttle goods across the checkpoints, by disguising taxable commodities as personal items. For instance, it is a common practice for commuters between Hong Kong and Shenzhen to buy two cans of infant milk powder before crossing the border and immediately sell them at nearby collecting points after the checkpoint. The price difference will neatly cover their transportation costs. This kind of player is commonly found in border regions around the world, for instance between India and Bangladesh (Pohit and Taneja 2000), Thailand and Laos (Elsing 2019), Benin and Nigeria (Flynn 1997), and Peru and Bolivia (Ødegaard 2008). They are considered petty traders because their scale of operation is usually very small.

Yet, further inquiry reveals the embedding relations behind the apparently solitary actors. A large number of related roles are involved, including not only solitary petty traders but also freelance as well as full-time couriers, and various professional actors such as brokers, drivers, porters, and shopkeepers, who work in an organized way. Other equally indispensable players include border guards, customs officials, police, and other public servants. Contrary to the common perception, genuinely solitary petty traders are actually a minority group. They have hitherto received the most attention because of their sheer number and their visibility. In reality, many apparently solitary traders are incorporated into larger trading networks without they themselves being aware of it. For example, when the petty Hong Kong traders sell their infant milk powder at collecting points in Shenzhen, little do they realize that they are taking part in a nationwide trading network of parallel goods in China.

Solitary players aside, the majority of individuals involved in shadow trade actually belong to an organized network, often formed between Chinese and foreign partners. They are recruited by organized syndicates to ferry goods across border checkpoints, either physically or as part of the headcount. Some work as freelancers, while others are full-time couriers. They are usually paid according to the quantity and value of goods they manage to get through customs. In Khorgos, for instance, on the eve of the pandemic, a courier received on average KZT3,000 (USD6.5) for ferrying a standard sized piece of Chinese merchandise weighing 25 kg (Fieldwork in Khorgos 2018). In comparison, couriers in Pogranichny receive around RUB600 (USD9) for carrying 25 kg of Chinese merchandise (Fieldwork in Pogranichny 2019).

The goods are assigned to them by specific group leaders or brokers shortly before departure.

All kinds of individuals are recruited into the organized networks. They are not merely confined to retirees or villagers in border towns. For instance, many non-local labourers work in Macao but reside on the other side of the border – Zhuhai – to take advantage of the lower housing costs. During their daily commute, many serve as couriers for smuggling syndicates. Subsequently, many mainland labourers choose to work in Macao not because the jobs are more attractive, but because their work permit allows them to cross the sub-border freely (Fieldwork in Macao 2022). Their shadow activities surged during the pandemic, when many syndicates moved their operations to Macao after the border lockdown in Hong Kong. To meet the rising domestic demand in mainland China due to the disruption in global logistics, Zhuhai children studying in Macao are recruited to carry parallel goods across the Zhuhai border as well (*Macau Daily* 17 June 2022).

Even more intriguing cases are reported in Kinshasa and Brazzaville, where smugglers made use of disabled wheelchair users to take advantage of their reduced fares in cross-border ferries. These disabled smugglers usually travelled on heavy tricycles which can carry several dozens of kilos of goods. Each would be accompanied by a team of shadow traders disguised as helpers to escape customs duties while taking care of the loading and unloading of goods during departure and arrival. Other smugglers made use of local youngsters who would jump into the water with their bundles of Chinese textiles on their backs as the ferry approached the Kinshasa River port. They escaped border checks by manoeuvring through the sewage tunnels and surfacing from manholes inside the city (Ayimpam 2015).

In these examples, individual players are organized into an operation network and they act in a coordinated way. While individual players come and go, join and exit the network in a casual and informal manner, the network itself is stable, resilient, and coordinated under an elaborate division of labour. Hung and Ngo (2019) call this 'organized informality'. It shows a high degree of sophistication in its coordination, with the syndicates in such networks overseeing the trade flow, responding to market signals, coordinating sourcing and distribution, arranging logistics, and co-opting/manipulating border control.

Corporate Actors

The second category comprises corporate actors. Many players involved in shadow exchanges are actually legal corporate entities. Needless to say, their degree of involvement differs. Some business firms merely provide such logistical services as transportation, storage, or container shipping to smugglers, albeit with their knowledge. Others take an active part in coordinating shadow operations. Some augment profit from their legal business with their shadow income; others use their formal licence as a camouflage for shadow businesses.

A good case in point is the franchised transportation companies in some border regions between China and its neighbouring countries. In South Korea, during the 2010s, for example, since China-bound ferry lines were only available in three Korean cities, namely Incheon, Pyengtaek, and Kunsan, the number of ferry crossings were limited. As a result, shuttle traders dominated these crossings and occupied almost half of the ferry seats from Incheon port and over three-quarters of the seats from Pyengtaek and Kunsan (Han et al. 2015: 441). Much as the shuttle traders depend on the ferry, so do the ferry companies depend on the traders. To maintain this symbiotic relation, the ferry companies offer discounted fares of up to 40–50 per cent of the normal rate to shuttle traders, hence promoting shadow exchange in an indirect way (Han et al. 2015: 441).

In the Heihe border in China, it was common before the pandemic to see ferries heading to Blagoveshchensk more or less exclusively filled with smugglers and shuttle traders. Each ferry, supposedly for passengers, would be loaded with tons of goods. The ferry schedule is at best nominal, because the actual departure and berthing depend on the congestion at the customs control. By coordinating with the smuggling syndicates and the customs authorities, the ferry company in practice facilitates a smooth flow of goods (Fieldwork in Heihe 2019).

A similar situation can be seen at the Pogranichny–Suifenhe border between Russia and China. Although the two checkpoints are just a kilometre apart, passengers are not allowed to cross the border on foot but are obliged to make use of the bus service offered by the three cartelized companies (Figure 4). Before the Covid-19 outbreak, there were twenty-five departures per day, and a total of 1,250 passengers were transported daily. In this set-up, tour operators who are closely associated with the bus companies monopolize the seats. The tour operators ensure that each bus trip is taken up by five groups of courier smugglers, each consisting of ten members, including a group leader. As soon as the Russian couriers cross to the Chinese side, a return bus loaded with Chinese goods stands waiting for them, ready for departure. The couriers then immediately head back to the Chinese customs for their return trip. In this operation, the franchised bus companies are directly involved in the organization of crowd smuggling (Fieldwork in Pogranichny and Suifenhe 2019).

An even more illustrative case of corporate actors can be found in the Sino-Kazakh shadow trade. The Khorgos International Centre, where most shadow exchanges take place, is located in the Saryesik-Atyrau Desert. The nearest city,

Figure 4 Shuttle bus delivering parallel goods from Suifenhe to Pogranichny.

Almaty, is five hours away by car. Most Kazakh shadow traders depend on bus services offered by tour agencies to reach Khorgos. Since the round trip is time-consuming and costly, traders would bring back as much merchandise as possible. On average, each trader takes back some 500 kg of merchandise, twenty times above the tax-free limit. Instead of paying an official penalty of EUR4 per extra kilo above the official 25 kg limit, a visitor may pay a bribe between KZT200 and KZT250 (approx. EUR0.4–EUR0.5) for each additional kilo to get through the Kazakh customs. This bribe, not paid directly to any customs officials, is collected by the tour operators who then distribute the money to several parties involved. Under this arrangement, there is no upper limit for the amount of goods a visitor can carry. Here the tour agencies perform a brokerage function between the border authorities and the smugglers. At the time of the fieldwork of this study in 2018, there were six licensed tour operators and around twenty unlicensed/illegal operators in Kazakhstan, all were private companies with good connections with the authorities. At each crossing, the tour agencies meticulously record the loading, report the headcount and loading to the customs, and pay the bribes on behalf of their tour members (Fieldwork in Almaty 2018).

In comparison with the shadow exchange in goods, an even more diverse variety of corporate actors can be found in shadow finance. Examples abound.

In Taiwan, many jewellery shops provide underground channels for customers who wish to send money in and out of China (Fieldwork in Taipei and Kaohsiung 2017). In Macao, besides the casino junkets, many massage salons and pawnshops also serve as hawaladars. In Hong Kong, some insurance companies offer high-premium life insurance policy schemes for their customers using UnionPay in mainland China. After the purchase, customers can immediately cash out their policies (with penalty) in Hong Kong currency and send the money to their preferred destinations. Even international auction houses can be unwitting participants in money laundering. An anonymous buyer may take part in an auction and buy a piece of art at an inflated price. The seller, who is part of the team, would then transfer the payment to an offshore account (*International Business Times* 21 February 2014).

Institutional Actors

The third category consists of institutional actors who are either state actors or public sector players. In other words, they are acting not as individual officials but on behalf of the collective interests of their public institutions. Observers have noted that states engage in shadow exchange for their own ends. States may rely on illicit flows to generate revenue; they may use shadow channels to procure prohibited items or technologies; or they may collaborate with shadow operators to exercise territorial control or maintain political authority (Kelman 2015). A state can therefore encourage, collude, or connive with shadow activities when it creates demand, provides supply, or facilitates the transaction of shadow exchange (Williams 1997).

State-sanctioned shadow exchange is not confined to 'rogue states' or 'mafia states' such as the case of Columbia, where the drug economy is deeply tied to state initiatives that aim at making spaces governable, expanding global trade, and attracting capital (Ballvé 2012). The scandal involving the Bank of Credit and Commerce International reveals that a number of governments and their intelligence services have made extensive use of the shadow financial services (Andreas 2011: 417). In the border town of Poipet, the Cambodian military ran all casinos in the previous decade. Like those in Macao, the Poipet casinos serve as channels of money laundering for Thai gamblers (Fieldwork in Poipet 2015). In Khorgos, all shadow goods that cannot be packed into the standard $60 \times 40 \times 20$ cm^3 boxes are obliged to use the state-run national postage service KazPost for delivery and inspection (Fieldwork in Almaty 2018). In essence, this gives KazPost an exclusive privilege to enjoy a piece of the pie in the crowd smuggling operation.

Mertha (2005) suggests that the Chinese state connives with counterfeit productions and piracy because the illicit industry is a major employer and growth engine. However, examples in China are not merely confined to state connivance. Instances of direct state engagement or collusion abound. The aforementioned case of the Yuanhua Group is a good example. When Yuanhua was busted, the entire Xiamen customs department was found to be associated with the smuggling empire. Customs officials were even included in the payroll of the Group. Besides local customs, the military in China was also once an active player. In 1985, the Chinese government decided to allow the military to run their own commercial business. The decision was made for the Chinese military to balance its own budget. As a result, various army bureaus and combat units established thousands of joint stock companies and shareholding companies in trade, transportation, entertainment, hotel, finance, and so on. Some units were directly involved in smuggling and trafficking (Goodman 1996). The policy was abandoned in 1998, but delinking the military from all profit-making activities was not completed until 2019.

Direct state involvement in overseas shadow operations is also evident. Chinese state banks have served as active partners of money launderers in Europe. In France, Italy, Luxemburg, and Spain, underground syndicates deposited stockpiles of cash derived from their smuggling into local branches of the Bank of China and ICBC. The banks set up a system and helped them remit hundreds of millions to China through fake identities and fraudulent invoices (*ProPublica* 31 July 2017)

In this regard, collusion between individuals, corporations, and state actors in their joint effort to organize shadow exchange is not uncommon. This can be found in Myanmar, where China together with the Burmese militia plays a key role in reconfiguring the northern Shan state from an area of armed resistance to a site of accumulation through shadow exchange (Meehan and Dan 2023). Chinese companies have partnered with narco-paramilitary organizations and militias in local investment projects, in essence embedding shadow exchange in their strategies of capital accumulation and local development (Woods 2019). Besides the inflow of Chinese capital into Burmese farmlands and mines as well as the outflow of Burmese timber, minerals, rare earth, oil, and gas to China, shadow trade of synthetic drugs such as ice (crystal methamphetamine) plays a big part. Before the 2010s, the production of ice was mainly concentrated in some coastal villages in Guangdong province, including the notorious Boshe village. The products were shipped to Taiwan, South Korea, Japan, and other Asian destinations. After the large-scale crackdowns by the Chinese authorities in 2013 and 2014, the production chain was moved to Shan state, with the ingredients supplied by Chinese syndicates based in Yunnan province. The drug economy operates under the protection of the militias, some of whom have been co-opted to work with the Burmese state in exchange for their continuous control of local territories and businesses. Interestingly, besides Chinese traders, Taiwanese syndicates are also involved, mainly in the manufacture of the synthetic drug and in delivering the end products to Taiwan, Malaysia, Indonesia, and the Philippines using fishing boats as the camouflage (*The Reporter* 12 July 2020).

Illicit technology transfer is another familiar area of collusive shadow operation among individual, corporate, and state actors. China has long been under the spotlight for this controversial practice (Hannas et al. 2013). A report by the Center for Strategic and International Studies (2023) recorded 224 Chinese espionage incidents against American firms and institutions since 2000, far outnumbering other countries. For instance, Chinese hackers infiltrated at least forty-eight chemical and defence companies to acquire sensitive military information in 2011. In 2014, Chinese hackers who targeted six American companies in the power, metal, and solar production industries were identified to be members of the People's Liberation Army. A recent economic/high-tech espionage charge involving the former Principal Engineer for Global Research at Coca-Cola, Xiarong You, is illustrative. Born in China, You obtained her PhD in the United States and became one of the limited number of employees at Coca-Cola (and later Eastman Chemical) who had exclusive access to trade secrets about BPA-free technology for the inside coating of food containers. The technology belongs to Akzo-Nobel, BASF, Dow Chemical, PPG, Toyochem, Sherwin Williams, and Eastman Chemical. You was recruited under the Thousand Talents Plan by the Chinese government, and stole the trade secrets for the Weihai Jinhong Group, a state enterprise owned by Shandong province. You was sentenced to fourteen years' imprisonment in 2022 for economic espionage and theft of trade secrets intended to benefit her China-based partner and the Chinese government.

All in all, people and organizations from all walks of life take part in shadow exchanges. They combine their formal role and position with their shadow job with ease. In some cases, the ostensible role is nothing more than a camouflage. In other cases, they engage in shadow exchange alongside their formal function. In some situations, shadow exchange is a moonlighting practice. In other situations, shadow exchange is the major source of revenue vis-à-vis formal income. Such a combination of formal–informal roles and the blend of open and shadow activities challenge not only the conception of a simplistic version of informality but also the conventional understanding of the formal economy. At a minimum, the formal and the informal are mutually embedded and constitutive of the modern economy. In the same vein, when state actors actively participate in illicit exchange, the line that supposedly separates law and authority on the one hand and criminal practices on the other is at best blurred. It confirms our earlier discussion that illicitness or illegality is largely a state construct.

Common Forms of Mass Shadow Practices

With the large number of individuals, corporations, and state actors taking part in shadow exchange, one may easily come to the conclusion that mass shadow exchanges are taking place at random. This cannot be further from the truth. In fact, notwithstanding the diversity of operational practices, the vast majority of those everyday smugglers, petty traders, and shadow brokers are unwitting links in the global value chains connected through shadow networks. This can be illustrated by the three common forms of mass operation that are employed by Chinese shadow networks, namely crowd smuggling, orchestrated petty trading, and surrogacy. They are most pervasive along China's borders, and have hitherto been mistakenly seen as uncoordinated and haphazard.

Crowd Smuggling

Crowd smuggling is by far the most representative type of mass shadow exchange. It can be found in most borders and is an illicit activity that involves ordinary people. The basic logic is the deployment of a large number of couriers or haulers to shuttle goods through the checkpoint, by disguising saleable goods as personal items so as to evade taxation. However, even in this kind of simple transaction, the modus operandi is more complicated than commonly understood.

Typically, couriers are recruited by organized syndicates to ferry the goods. Many of them are local residents of border communities who make use of their border pass to carry out the smuggling. In most cases, the syndicates are essentially third-party service providers – that is, they act like a logistics company. Owners of the goods will pay a certain service fee to a syndicate to shuttle their goods across border checkpoints. The syndicate will collect the goods, entrust them to its dealers (who in turn will recruit couriers), coordinate the border passage, and deliver the goods to assigned destinations. The main difference between crowd smuggling and a legal logistics operation lies in the way goods are exported. Instead of being shipped in one consignment, the goods are hand-carried across the border in small quantities by thousands of couriers, and then reassembled for delivery on the other side of the border.

The operation at the Hong Kong–Shenzhen border can be seen as a typical example. Crowd smugglers from Shenzhen arrive at the Sheung Shui metro station in Hong Kong every day. Guided by a team leader, they then head in groups to several industrial buildings in the nearby district. Dozens of stockrooms run by different syndicates are housed in the industrial buildings. Every morning the goods are delivered by trucks and loaded into the stockrooms. The operation resembles a Fordist production line: trucks deliver goods to the industrial buildings; workers unload wagons of goods to different stockrooms;

couriers stuff their suitcases with goods in the hallways; dealers in each stockroom give instructions to couriers about what products to take and in what quantity (Figure 5). Once the couriers receive their goods, they head back immediately to the border checkpoint. After the border control, they hand in the goods at specific collection points near the border gate. The collector will pay them on the spot after inspecting the condition and quantity of the goods. The couriers then head back to Hong Kong for another round of operation. In the meantime, the collector gathers the goods from a number of couriers before transporting them to nearby warehouses for stock taking and repackaging. After that, the products are delivered either to the entrusting agents/owners, to shops specializing in Hong Kong goods, or to other retail outlets in the rest of the country (Hung and Ngo 2019).

There are two central concerns in this mode of operation: freight volume and risk. A number of constraining factors limit the 'freight volume' of crowd smuggling. They include the frequency of transportation, number of couriers, and luggage allowance. These factors vary from checkpoint to checkpoint, even with checkpoints in relative proximity. For instance, at the Suifenhe crossing, a strict weight limit is imposed on hand-carried goods, and every traveller is required to obtain a weight clearance before passing through customs. Control

Figure 5 Couriers picking up goods at a Sheung Shui stockroom in Hong Kong.

is less stringent at the Dongning–Poltavka crossing, which is a mere 50 km away from Suifenhe within the same Heilongjiang province (Fieldwork in Suifenhe and Poltavka 2019). Other restrictions abound. For instance, at the Hong Kong–Shenzhen border, couriers are allowed to commute only twice a day. Warning signals will go off when commuters pass the automatic gateway for the third time, resulting in thorough checks and interrogation by customs authorities. Furthermore, on the metro line connecting passengers to the border checkpoint, only one piece of luggage per passenger is allowed, the size of which should not exceed 170 cm (length + width + height in total) and 23 kg in weight. To overcome these constraints, a large number of couriers are recruited, usually through chain referrals (Fieldwork in Hong Kong 2015).

In Pogranichny, constraints arise from a different source. As mentioned earlier, with only twenty-five shuttle bus departures per day heading for the Chinese border, the total number of couriers is therefore limited to 1,250, regardless of how many recruits a syndicate enlists. Each hauler is allowed to carry 25 kg of goods. In order to maximize the freight volume, crowd smugglers have to occupy all bus seats. This in essence turns the passenger port into a cargo port where bona fide visitors and tourists have little chance of obtaining bus tickets (Fieldwork in Pogranichny 2019). The same logic applies to the ports of Blagoveshchensk, Incheon, Pyengtaek, and Kunsan, where ferry crossings are dominated by crowd smugglers.

In response to these kinds of constraints, crowd smugglers adapt their activities. This was seen in the operation at the Dongxing–Móng Cái border before the Covid-19 lockdown. While there is no size or weight restrictions for luggage passing through the checkpoints, the use of trolleys is prohibited. Couriers hand-carry the goods up the stairs to reach the Dongxing checkpoint (Figure 6). The total value of goods for each crossing is restricted at this checkpoint, although no restriction is placed on the number of crossings. Because of that, crowd smugglers cross the border as many times as possible, each time carrying a small quantity of goods with limited value. However, such ‘border crossing’ is only for half the way because after leaving the border control on the Chinese side, Chinese couriers dump their goods at collecting points on the footbridge connecting the two border customs, and immediately head back to pick up another batch of goods. This half-way crossing vastly reduces the crossing time since the Chinese couriers do not have to pass through the Vietnamese border control. The footbridge there is an ambiguous zone that serves the smugglers conveniently (Figure 7). The goods deposited on the footbridge are picked up by the couriers’ Vietnamese accomplices from the Vietnam side. In a similar way, the Vietnamese couriers return to Móng Cái as soon as they pick up the deposited goods in the ambiguous zone. The whole

Figure 6 Crowd smugglers heading to the Dongxing checkpoint.

Figure 7 Footbridge in Sino-Vietnamese border serving as a drop-and-pick area.

operation relies on synchronized crossing times so that the two circuits of flow overlap at specific hours of the day (Fieldwork in Móng Cái 2019). All these creative adaptations demonstrate the entrepreneurial quality of crowd smugglers who successfully achieve economies of scale to minimize their operating costs.

The second concern of crowd smuggling is risk. Common scenarios include couriers running away with valuable goods, border authorities confiscating the goods, and heavy penalties levied on prohibited goods that are intercepted. In contrast to the conventional belief about the centrality of social trust in shadow exchange, the possibility of couriers absconding with the entrusted goods is always high. This is particularly so when a large number of couriers, including strangers, are recruited through social media such as Facebook and WeChat. To prevent them from going astray, dealers may jot down the couriers' personal information such as mobile phone number, residence ID, passport number, and so on; use referrals by someone already in the network; or even deploy underground gangs as deterrence (Wang 2017).

Some other strategies are used by syndicates to reduce risks. One common practice is to distribute goods of different value evenly among the couriers to avoid putting all eggs in one basket. In Khorgos, dealers even use portable barcode scanners to register the goods assigned to individual couriers. Couriers would have to present the printed receipt together with the goods to the collector on the Chinese side of the border (Fieldwork in Khorgos 2018). In many instances, couriers are organized into groups and are supervised by group leaders in their movement. For the smuggling of valuable goods such as machine parts, mobile phones, precious metals, and banknotes, syndicates usually rely on closed networks of couriers whom they know personally. In Heihe, the local Russian mafia is deployed to ferry precious metals to Blagoveshchensk (Fieldwork in Heihe 2019).

For the couriers, they face a different kind of risk. Most of the time they are not fully aware of the content of the packages that they carry. In particular, they have little idea of the licitness of those goods wrapped in boxes. There was a case in Hong Kong when a courier was jailed for seven years for carrying twelve airsoft guns into China. The courier claimed that he was paid HKD500 (USD65) to carry some electronic components and that he had no idea about the guns (*Apple Daily* 18 May 2017).

Periodic crackdowns by the border authorities constitute another source of risk. Experienced smugglers will alter their trajectory of movement in response to changes in the control routines to circumvent possible blockage. Couriers tend to move in groups to watch each other's backs. The leader of each group will report unexpected encounters at the checkpoints to the head broker, so that groups behind can adjust their movements. In times when checks are tightened or when border control is on high alert, trade syndicates will suspend their activities altogether. The ability to assess the potential and extent of risks thus enables experienced smugglers to successfully navigate their passage in this highly securitized space.

Orchestrated Petty Trading

A variant of crowd smuggling relies on an open network of traders. Unlike the already-mentioned operation in which syndicates recruit couriers to ferry goods, the syndicates in this kind of operation make use of individual petty traders to do the job. It is an ingenious operation in which risks are passed on to individual traders. It remains the dominant form of operation at the Macao–Zhuhai border even during the pandemic, and a popular form at the Hong Kong–Shenzhen border. As aforementioned, many commuters take advantage of their routine crossing to smuggle a small amount of taxable goods. The operation is facilitated by the presence of a large number of shops in the proximity of the border gates in Hong Kong and Macao, specializing in parallel products. Each product is marked with two prices: a selling price and a slightly higher, indicative re-purchasing price offered by specific shops in Shenzhen and Zhuhai. The price difference constitutes the potential profit for a commuter who buys and sells an item. In this regard, the shops dictate the range of goods to be ferried across the border. The activity is further facilitated by the presence of buyers hanging around the customs building, offering to buy the goods. These buyers are in essence collectors, because they merely buy the items on behalf of their trading network. Each of them buys specific sets of goods and delivers them to collection points that are in turn linked to nationwide distribution networks (Fieldwork in Macao 2021).

This is essentially a kind of orchestrated operation. Syndicates make use of independent petty traders to circumvent checkpoint control, without the need to establish any reciprocal relationship with them. Although shops selling parallel goods run the risk of being busted from time to time, the syndicates do not have to pay the cost of labour for ferrying the goods across the border. They do not have to worry that couriers will run away with the entrusted goods because the shops selling the goods have already cashed in. Nor will they face any risk of being intercepted by customs. However, this form of operation has its limitations. Since individual petty traders are basically walk-in customers, the syndicates have no control over their number and frequency of visits. For operations involving valuable items, items in huge quantities, and delivery within a certain time frame, the use of courier smuggling is more effective (Hung and Ngo 2019).

Surrogacy

Another variant of crowd smuggling is surrogacy. It is a rather unique form of shadow exchange that has become very popular in China. In this operation, people purchase specific foreign products through a surrogate shopper without paying import tax and, very often, sales tax. Before the pandemic, millions of Chinese travellers and sojourners visiting various countries as tourists, overseas students, contract labours, professionals, and businessmen provided the human resources needed for this operation. In the beginning, most of them started as freelance surrogate shoppers who receive orders through social media, chat groups, or Internet platforms, purchasing the items in Hong Kong or elsewhere on behalf of their clients, and sending the products to their clients through courier or postal service (Fieldwork in Hong Kong 2015). It is in essence a combination of suitcase trade and e-commerce. The most popular foreign products for surrogate shopping include cosmetics, infant milk powder, bags and luggage cases, hats and shoes, electronic products, and luxury watches and jewellery (China E-commerce Research Centre 2010).

Surrogate shopping has grown exponentially in recent years, thanks to the advancement of the Internet, courier logistics, and social media. The major actors have shifted from petty shoppers to large transnational syndicates. China is once again the centre of surrogate smuggling. The practice of syndicates based in Hong Kong and mainland China is illustrative of its modus operandi. These syndicates receive orders from WeChat in mainland China and organize regular trips from Hong Kong to Paris, Tokyo, and Seoul. Typically, for a seven-day shopping trip, a syndicate would recruit shoppers to travel to Paris and pay for their airfare and accommodation. Similar to the function of a hauler in crowd smuggling, the shopper is hired mainly for the head count. The actual shopping is done by the core members of the syndicate. The shoppers station themselves in the department stores mainly to claim tax refunds applicable to non-EU tourists. They also have to queue up in high-street stores to buy limited edition brand-name bags with purchase limits. Besides getting free airfare and hotel accommodation, each shopper earns HKD1500 (USD190) for three days' work plus a few days' free time for his/her own sightseeing or shopping. Each would have some eight boxes of merchandise registered under his/her name on the return flight. The shoppers also receive a commission of around HKD800 (USD100) per box on successful delivery. After arrival in Hong Kong, the goods are shuttled by crowd smuggling to mainland China for delivery to specific clients (Fieldwork in Hong Kong 2017).

The cost of such organized surrogate shopping is fairly high, but the profit margin is equally handsome. In a single Paris trip, no less than USD0.5 million worth of goods are procured. The operation is facilitated by department stores in the West that embrace such bulk buying. In Paris, Chinese-speaking sales staff are recruited in many department stores to cater for the needs of the shoppers. In Tokyo, some department stores devote a whole section to help shoppers process tax refunds. They even provide special facilities and staff to help package the purchased goods (Fieldwork in Tokyo 2018).

In sum, the wide range of mass shadow practices described here underline the intricate divisions of labour and coordination in shadow exchange, which are often thought to be casual, ad hoc, and haphazard. Depending on the commodities, trade routes, and border situations, transnational shadow exchanges vary in terms of professionalization and organizational sophistication. Each illicit network has its own division of labour, reflecting its distinctive layers of differential power and dependency.

Such 'organized informality', combined with the involvement of multiple actors cooperating in various formal and informal capacities, creates highly flexible operations that enable Chinese shadow networks to grow and expand. During this process, thousands of local, solitary, petty traders are unknowingly incorporated into larger transnational shadow networks. Together they play indispensable roles in the global shadow chains. This global–local link constitutes a new turn in globalization that has far-reaching implications for the global political economy.

5 Grey Governance in Shadow Globalization

The global expansion of Chinese shadow networks and the rise of China's shadow power have dramatically changed the nature of the global value chains. This has in turn led to an alternative spatial division of labour where previously peripheral regions are now integrated into the shadow world. Along the Belt and Road countries, in particular, numerous corporate and state actors have intentionally or unintentionally facilitated this integration through active collusion or tacit toleration. The overall result is a new turn in globalization, in which the shadow side plays an increasingly prominent role.

This has led researchers to speak of illicit globalization (Andreas 2011, 2015), deviant globalization (Gilman et al. 2013), underground globalization (Zook 2003), shadow globalization (Jung 2003), or low-end globalization (Mathews et al. 2017). Researchers differ in their understanding of the shadow process as merely an underside of a single ongoing globalization process or as a parallel alternative. They also disagree over the consequences. Some argue that the global shadow exchange undermines state power, others suggest that the relationship is symbiotic rather than antagonistic. Some regard it as a challenge to neoliberal globalization and the hegemonic position of the West, others warn against overstating the emancipatory role of such alternative globalization and the leverage acquired by the hitherto marginalized people in the periphery.

These are big questions that can only be answered in the long term. Suffice it to say here that the macro-historical implications of shadow exchange can only be understood when the discrete, mosaic operations are brought together in the analysis. In this regard, analysing global China as a structuring factor will be instrumental to our understanding.

Governing Transborder Movements

Since modern states have securitized national boundaries, most border crossings are allowed only at specific gateways or checkpoints that are heavily guarded. In such circumstances, transnational shadow exchange is possible only when the fluidity and ambiguity of borders are fully exploited. The Belt and Road routes would not have served as the infrastructural pathways for shadow networks if border crossings were strictly controlled. The negotiation of transborder passage is therefore a key concern for smugglers.

Existing scholarship tends to attribute border passage to the existence of grey areas in border control, in particular the ability of smugglers to exploit grey areas through corruption and patronage (see, for example, Elsing 2019; Mahanty 2019). A vast literature thus focuses on the obstacles, asymmetries, materialities, and manoeuvres involved in the act of border crossing (Sur 2013). Analysing the multiple interactions during border passage, researchers have coined neologisms such as ‘bordering practices’ (Parker and Adler-Nissen 2012), ‘borderwork’ (Rumford 2012), ‘borderities’ (Amilhat-Szary and Giraut 2015), and ‘borderscapes’ (Brambilla 2015) to capture the dynamic and contentious processes.

Notwithstanding the extreme securitization of border control, its effectiveness is shaped by many factors, including state policies, bilateral relations, bureaucratic competence, local/borderland practices, and in situ adaptation (Plümmer 2022). In many borderlands, the state and smugglers may assume a less antagonistic and more symbiotic relationship. Governance is achieved through negotiations and compromises among state and non-state actors, including militias, intermediate groups, and outlawed forces or terrorists (Su 2018: 23). This is most notable in border regions along the Belt and Road Initiative, where forms of grey governance, or what van Schendel (2005) called ‘everyday transnationality’, can be found in the running of transborder units.

This symbiotic governance cannot be reduced to corruption. Conventional bribery exchange typically takes place between individual parties whose relationship is particularistic and often secretive. The terms of corrupt exchange are often ad hoc if not arbitrary; they are negotiated case by case, situation by situation. Such forms of corrupt exchange have serious limitations when applied to border crossing. Most border checkpoints are manned by a large number of officials, all carrying out checks under panoptical surveillance (Jeganathan 2018). Corrupt exchange between border guards and the large number of traders cannot rely on spot transactions on an individual basis. It has to be organized.

Organized corruption during border crossing means that bribes are neither casual nor arbitrary. The price is agreed upon beforehand and there must be a way by which the amount is calculated and delivered. How these bribes are to be paid, by whom, to whom, and how they are divided among the recipients have to be understood and agreed upon by the actors. Such organized corruption has been documented in case studies. In Guangzhou, counterfeits and knockoffs destined for Africa were sent through specific logistics agents who bribed customs agents in advance. They paid CNY300 (approx. USD50) for every 3 m^3 of illicit goods in a container, or CNY3,000–4,000 (approx. USD500–600) for a container with a large quantity of counterfeits. When occasional anti-piracy campaigns were launched by customs, the logistics agents would be alerted in advance (Mathews 2015: 425–6). In the Hekou–Lào Cai border between China's Yunnan province and Vietnam, huge volumes of duty-free Chinese products were shuttled into Vietnam every day before the Covid-19 outbreak. Special border-crossing permits allow border residents to carry items up to VND2 million (USD87) per day. Many traders, however, ferry goods far exceeding this amount by paying a monthly bribe to customs officials and market control teams. During night-time, well-connected criminal gangs move goods almost freely, except for drug and human trafficking (Endres 2014: 617).

Corrupt exchange at the border checkpoint therefore exhibits regularity, with impersonal and uniform terms of exchange that are open secrets, applicable to old and new players. It involves widely recognized and impersonal rules and practices that are observed by the participants. It is essentially a governance regime, albeit informal in nature. In general, informal governance predicates on socially shared – but often unwritten – rules that are created, communicated, and enforced outside the officially sanctioned channels (Helmke and Levitsky 2004: 727). It emerges as a coping strategy to overcome complex bureaucratic arrangements (Reh 2012), as a way of bypassing obsolete or impractical rules (Gel'man 2004), as a means to solve collective action problems and reduce transaction costs (Kleine 2013), or as a practical mode of everyday governance that is formed, contested, and negotiated on the street, in the market, and at the borders (Hagmann and Péclard 2010: 530).

Grey governance at the borders is distinctive in two regards. First of all, the set-up relies not only on the active participation of state actors but also on the willingness of the smugglers and their supporting agents to play along. In other words, it is the involvement of multiple actors of the state and society, with their symbiotic relationships, which contributes to the formation of a governance regime. Second, the rules and practices are not just informal but also outlawed by the state itself. Practices including bribery, tax evasion, and smuggling are punishable by law.

The workings of grey governance can be best illustrated with the case of Khorgos, the main crossroad in the Belt and Road project. The key role that tour operators play is that of brokering agents who organize the bribes paid by traders to the border authorities. Besides the tour operators, there is a long chain of players in the grey governance regime. They include the customs, the military, the regional administration, and the franchised transport companies. Each group of players assumes a specific role in the grey governance regime, and together they work out a division of labour that, on the one hand, ensures a smooth running of the regime and, on the other hand, shares the bribes/crossing fees in a mutually agreed proportion (Fieldwork in Khorgos 2018).

The grey governance regime in Khorgos does not operate in secrecy but runs parallel to the formal border control regime. Elsewhere Anders (2010: 132) notes that a 'parallel order' emerges where government bureaucracies use informal arrangements to bridge the gap between formal rules and actual practices. It is a modus vivendi that replaces those formal rules which are too far removed from the situation on the ground. Yet this parallel order in Khorgos goes beyond what Anders described. To facilitate implementation, all merchandise has to be packed in a standardized format to allow for a speedy calculation of crossing fees (Figure 8). In response to this requirement, a vibrant business has emerged in the proximity of the customs area to provide packaging, weighing, and storage services. A mark is made on goods to indicate those for which the 'crossing fees' are arranged through the tour operator-cum-broker. Customs officials only have to count the total number of pieces belonging to a particular tour operator to know the appropriate crossing fees. There is no negotiation at the customs checkpoint, since bribes from individual traders are not accepted. For unmarked packages, the items would be thoroughly checked, weighed, and recorded in the official system. The formal rules would then apply; and the respective owners would have to pay the official customs duties (Fieldwork in Khorgos 2018). In other words, the two parallel orders do not function separately. They are, in Olivier de Sardan's (2015: 26) words, 'superimposed, interwoven and entangled'.

Figure 8 After customs clearance, goods packed in standardized size heading for Almaty and the rest of Central Asia.

Because of that, border control exhibits a new dimension under grey governance. The rules and practices are enforced by a multitude of actors whose informal functions deviate from their ostensible formal roles, with a division of labour trespassing the public–private divide. There are two parallel customs and excise practices, forming a kind of 'institutional symbiosis' where a visible, formal institutional façade covers an invisible, informal core of a shadow economy (Gel'man 2012: 139).

Grey governance exists not only in border control but also in shadow outlets along the Belt and Road routes. This can be seen in Central Asia, where many bazaars were once associated with crime and chaos as a result of the institutional void created by the post-Soviet transition. Yet traders, owners, and officials join hands in a fluid and crisis-ridden context to define and establish informal governance of the bazaars. The Dordoi Bazaar in Bishkek is illustrative. It is a central hub in the Eurasian shadow trading networks. Spector (2017) finds that traders adapt Soviet experiences and pre-Soviet practices in post-Soviet, market-based settings to create islands of order at Dordoi. The stakeholders engage in political negotiation, adapt pre-existing ideas and organizational practices, recompose institutions, and reconstitute them with new meanings and practices. The situation resembles what Cleaver (2015: 209) describes as institutional bricolage, when people draw on existing repertoires of social norms and traditions to assemble arrangements and adapt the practices to new challenges.

For traders and smugglers, their main goal is to maximize cost-effectiveness and minimize risk during border crossing. They do not care whether the fees are tax duties or bribes, nor do they mind if the money goes to private purses rather than the state treasury. Their primary concern is the predictability of rules and prices, which will allow them to calculate their costs and to carry out their shadow activities in a planned manner. In fact, paying bribes is often cheaper and more convenient than following official regulations, as long as the graft is regular and calculable. The Khorgos case shows that the grey regime is actually less extractive than the official regime itself. Traders are more than happy to pay bribes – to avoid the official penalty which is ten times the bribe – for goods that exceed the legally approved limit. In Africa, traders regard bribing customs officials as a way of life. The real concern for most traders is unpredictability, that the bribery payment may vary from one consignment to another (Mathews 2015: 430).

From the perspective of border officials, they ensure that they balance multiple state policies, the orderly passage of goods and people, and that they reap some personal benefits from the set-up. Brokers and smugglers thus collude with state gatekeepers for preferential passage and information on border control. In return, gatekeeping officials count on brokers for the coordination of movements through the checkpoints in an orderly manner. It is a delicate symbiotic relationship, characterized by periodic tensions and conflicts, leading to a kind of 'border games' or 'collaborative scheme' (Andreas 2000). It also reminds us of the insights of Heyman and Smart (1999: 7) about the interactive processes and practices of the state–illegal practice nexus. Unlike rules and structures, such practices allow room for indeterminacy, ambiguity, and double-dealing. This symbiotic nexus explains why irregular activities can proliferate in highly regulated space, and why states choose to tolerate illegality. In the end, legality and illegality are 'simultaneously black and white, and shades of gray' (Heyman and Smart 1999: 11).

Checkpoint Politics

The functionality of grey governance allows many shadow exchanges to take place in broad daylight and in front of the border authorities. Nevertheless, there is often a tacit understanding about the limit of such activities. One obvious limit is the smuggling of objectionable products. Detection of such products will often invite high-handed measures from the authorities that may jeopardize the entire shadow operation. What constitutes an objectionable product is however contingent on local circumstances and state policies. Dangerous items such as drugs, firearms, and precious metals are usually on the forbidden list, but other items such as electronic cigarettes, mobile phones, or dried seafood may also be restricted. At the Sino-Russian border, the smuggling of sea cucumber is severely punished. During fieldwork, a female courier was thoroughly searched by the Pogranichny border control and subsequently detained for attempting to smuggle a pack of sea cucumber into China. The discovery of a blacklisted item puts the customs officials on high alert. Such news rapidly spread to the smuggling syndicates, resulting in the cancellation of all crowd smuggling activities in the days that follow (Fieldwork in Pogranichny 2019). In general, border authorities do carry out crackdowns from time to time. This serves a number of purposes: to remind shadow traders who is in charge, to restrain excessive trade, to punish those who test the limits of permissibility, and to show to the wider public that the state is in control. In essence, grey governance delimits the parameters of manoeuvre within which shadow exchange can take place.

In this regard, shadow traders' entrepreneurial skills and learned experiences prove to be essential during border crossing. The different modi operandi in crowd smuggling, surrogate shopping, hawala transfer, and so on are illustrative of the various strategies deployed to escape border control. For instance, in the crowd smuggling between Hong Kong and Shenzhen, the syndicates change their hordes of couriers every few months. Although this means that the syndicates will have to reorganize their networks frequently, the arrangement reduces the risk of their couriers being recognized by customs control, hence reducing the chance of being intercepted (Hung and Ngo 2019). Experienced smugglers alter their paths of movement swiftly in response to changes in the control routines or the flow of people and goods at specific checkpoints. When Hong Kong tightened its border control with Shenzhen during the Covid-19 pandemic, crowd smugglers immediately turned to the neighbouring Macao–Zhuhai border (Fieldwork in Macao and Zhuhai 2021). In Central Africa, studies find that smugglers and border guards engage in a cat-and-mouse game. At the Kinshasa–Brazzaville border, for example, traffickers use dugout canoes and small jetty boats for easy access to improvised piers. They simply move the boarding spot to a new location soon after detection (Ayimpam 2015: 395). In general, experienced smugglers will synthesize and synchronize different timetables and schedules – such as timetables of trains and shipments as well as rosters and work shift schedules of border guards and customs – to maximize efficiency and minimize risks (Ngo and Hung 2019).

It is through synthesizing pieces of disjunctive information, skilfully exploiting the time–space dynamics, and cautiously manipulating the rules of the grey governance regime that experienced, entrepreneurial shadow traders survive the risky operations. Their ability to utilize price signals, market incentives, organizational resources, innovative strategies, and entrepreneurial skills is comparable to formal business firms. Such skills and qualities make them the agents of this new phase of globalization.

In the same vein, effective border governance in the wake of massive shadow activities depends on the state authorities' skilful manipulation of the formal and informal regimes. The intertwining of the two games constitutes a technology of rule with which local authorities can exert their control and power (Ngo 2023). By selectively enforcing formal customs rules and informal practices at different time–space conjunctures, border authorities maintain a precarious balance between flexible adaptation and the rigid sovereign authority of the state. This explains the apparent unevenness of state power across different borders and at different times. Some border checkpoints are therefore strictly regulated, while others are loosely controlled; while the same checkpoint can be highly restrictive at one time but relatively relaxed at another. Seen from this perspective, the lack of uniformity and consistency in border governance is anything but a failure of the state. On the contrary, it is a ruling strategy that contributes to the adaptiveness of checkpoint politics.

Shadow Link in the Global Value Chain

For a long time, economic globalization has been driven by multinationals of the West who benefited from the neoliberal logic of capitalist expansion. The flow of global resources is dominated by inter- and intra-firm exchanges in the forms of capital, information, knowledge, strategy, plans, and personnel. The organizational power and strategic know-how of multinationals allow them to control the global value chains. Such dominant control is now partly contested by shadow exchange spearheaded by informal networks, many of which are connected to a global China.

Those transnational shadow networks – formed by traders, sojourners, bazaar owners, hawaladars, couriers and haulers, and smugglers – manage an alternative transnational flow of capital and commodity. As Mathews (2011: 19–20) puts it, it is globalization carried out by ordinary people, with limited capital and resources, but no less remarkable in establishing long-distance, intercontinental connections through a combination of formal and informal means. At the same time, the circulation of shadow products, including counterfeits and knockoffs through informal channels, has achieved a penetrative reach to encompass peripheral areas in the world. By bringing affordable consumables to these lands, the clandestine trade helps put the once-marginalized regions of the world back on the map and enable their people to enjoy the fruits of globalization (Mathews 2015). This leads some observers to characterize transnational shadow exchange as a kind of 'low-end globalization' (Mathews et al. 2017) or 'globalization from below' (Mathews et al. 2012).

In this sense, the global–local link in the transnational shadow networks has given the underprivileged groups a new leverage, a niche to bypass the formal rules which have hitherto been stacked against them. As shown in earlier discussions, many of the players are relentless entrepreneurs who exhibit sophisticated coordination capacity in their search for new market niches. They are, as Gilman et al. (2013:7) suggest, the most audacious experimenters, risk-takers, and innovators in today's global economy. In doing so, they mobilize resources and create profits that contribute significantly to local development, especially for border communities. This stands in contrast to the professional transnational criminal groups who engage in arm sales, human trafficking, drug trade, and so on. Observers have often regarded the latter as pathological and parasitic because they endanger social order and divert valuable resources to unproductive uses.

In this regard, the term 'low-end globalization' is somewhat misleading since it gives the impression that only low-value merchandise is exchanged through small-scale petty trade. This stereotypical impression cannot be further from reality. In fact, all sorts of goods and services are involved in transnational shadow exchanges. Various scales of operation, both small and large, can be found. Some operations are highly sophisticated in terms of their logistical coordination and divisions of labour. In the same vein, the term 'globalization from below' can be equally misleading. It carries the connotation that only the common people are involved. However, as the earlier discussion has shown, many corporations and state actors are also playing an integral part in this globalization process, not only in terms of collusion and connivance, but also as active agents who embrace the process for their own benefits (Kelman 2015). Even institutional infrastructures are created, in the form of grey governance, to facilitate the whole process. It is therefore not a process driven exclusively from below, although it differs from the earlier phase of globalization when common people, especially those from the poor regions, were excluded from taking part directly.

Such a new turn in globalization has further implications for the spatial division of labour. So far, the coordination of worldwide processes of production, distribution, and accumulation have taken place through city networks and global value chains. Major cities in the West such as New York, London,

Frankfurt, and Tokyo are connected by interlocking networks and intra-firm flows among multinationals in the advanced producer service sector. These cities therefore serve as nodal centres for different commodity chains by providing services for sourcing, producing, and distributing goods. In doing so, the uneven distribution of spatial power sustains an international division of labour between the global command centres of advanced capitalist countries and those on the peripheries (Brenner et al. 2010).

In the shadow turn in globalization, the centre of gravity has shifted towards the South, especially towards China. By taking part in alternative networks of informal connectivity or by hooking up shadow operations with existing value chains, the once-peripheral regions have emerged as nodal centres of long-distance resource flows. Cities such as Yiwu, Guangzhou, Khorgos, Dordoi, Ussuriysk, Sost, and Nairobi are now connected to one another in a different world city network. The pathways of shadow flows are determined not only by border situations but also by the host countries' domestic circumstances which generate opportunities for shadow entrepreneurs (Gilman et al. 2013: 5). In this alternative spatial division of labour, all roads lead to China, by virtue of its multiple roles in shadow exchange. China has emerged as the coordinating centre for many shadow networks and as the creator of numerous shadow links in the global value chain. While it may be a stretch to view this development as a challenge to the existing structure of global domination under neoliberalism (Evans 2008), it does bring new variables to transnational resource flow because the end markets for global value chains are no longer exclusively located in Europe and North America (Gereffi 2014).

In particular, the role played by shadow exchange at the downstream end of global value chains deserves attention. Multinationals are increasingly outsourcing their non-core production and service activities, resulting in a fragmentation of production but integration of trade (Feenstra 1998). The coordination of such fragmented activities has become a major concern (Gereffi et al. 2005). While the governance of the tiers of suppliers in production is less of a problem, the coordination of the distribution chain proves challenging, especially if the end markets are moving away from the West. Many markets in the developing world are characterized by the absence of reliable distribution channels, weak marketing platforms, prevalence of counterfeit products, phony sales practices, and so on.

Take China as an example, the distribution sector was liberalized in 2004 when foreign companies were allowed to apply for national wholesale and retail licences. Yet the actual practice remains complicated. For instance, in the market for foreign infant formula milk, no fewer than four tiers of agents and distributors are involved: first, the exclusive agent of the China region, followed by the provincial distributors, then the district or county distributors, and finally the retail shops (Hung and Ngo 2019). In such a fragmented and redundant system, layers of costs are added to the retail price, notwithstanding the high import tariffs. Worse still, multiple channels and vendors exist side by side, making competing claims for their exclusive rights to represent an international brand (Feuling 2010). It is difficult for ordinary consumers to verify the authenticity of self-claimed entrusted retailers.

In such circumstances, many Chinese consumers put their faith in products coming directly from Hong Kong and Macao, even if they are parallel goods. International brands take advantage of this convenient distribution channel via Hong Kong and Macao. Instead of increasing their direct exports to China, multinationals simply increase their export volume to Hong Kong and Macao, and let the suitcase traders take care of their distribution (Hung and Ngo 2019: 240). As a result, many international brands have been tolerant of the shadow activities in China since they are benefiting from the local distribution network. Nor do they protest strongly about copy goods since the markets for genuine products and for counterfeits are quite separate. For the established brands, counterfeit sales do not really cut into their profits because these involve aspirational items mainly among low-end consumers (Mathews 2015: 432), who may even boost the popularity of an established brand. At the same time, genuine goods 'exported' to China through informal trade simply help to raise their sales volume. The loss in import tax merely affects the state treasury, and it has few implications for the multinationals.

Although this practice is most prominent in luxury consumables, it also applies to all kinds of products and even industrial components. For instance, some manufacturers source their legally produced IC components from abroad and ship them to Hong Kong or Macao through formal channels. These components are then smuggled to mainland China via suitcase trade. The components are used to manufacture knockoff mobile phones. Some enterprises rely mostly on shadow finance for their operation capital and hire informal workers in their production. The finished products are subsequently exported to South Asia, Central Asia, and Russia through smuggling networks. In the process, the global value chain is long and effectively connected, thanks to a combination of legal and shadow practices.

The presence of shadow links in the global value chain shows that the so-called illicit, underground, or deviant globalization is not a parallel process running in competition with the normal, licit globalization. Quite the opposite, the mass shadow process has become part and parcel of mainstream globalization. Traders often engage in open and shadow transactions at the same time. Legal and forbidden goods are often mixed together in transnational trade, under the same consignment, trade route, and supply chain. Counterfeits are combined with genuine products in their shipments; liquors are camouflaged among soya sauce bottles; and mobile phones are hidden under machine parts. Licit and illicit funds flow through the same global banking system and are sheltered in the same offshore financial havens. Different parts of commodity production and distribution are assembled together through both open and shadow ways. Multinationals source their supplies from both licit and illicit ends. In short, licit and illicit exchanges are deeply embedded and mutually intertwined.

Since the divide between the licit and illicit within contemporary globalization is blurred, such terms as illicit globalization, deviant globalization, and underground globalization can be confusing because they give the impression that there is a separate shadow process running parallel to mainstream globalization. In reality, it is a shadow that cannot be detached or separated from the broader process of globalization (Gilman et al. 2013).

For this reason, this new turn in globalization is not necessarily antagonistic to the existing structure of global capitalism. In many instances, shadow exchange fills a void in the formal global value chain by offering an alternative arrangement that is more effective and trustworthy, despite its shadowy nature. But neither is it necessarily an emancipating alternative. Similar to mainstream globalization, hierarchies of power and domination exist in the shadow side. Van Schendel (2020) points out that the most precarious actors are the casual labourers, couriers, porters, and cart-pushers. Higher up in the power hierarchy are the suitcase traders, drivers, and brokers. The tour operators, independent entrepreneurs, and shop owners are even further up in the echelons. The top positions are occupied by syndicates and franchised companies that coordinate voluminous flows of the clandestine trade, and state officials who assist in the border passage. Which individuals occupy what commanding heights depends on the positionality of particular actors and their place in the creation of asymmetric interdependencies (Sheppard 2002). In the end, similar exploitative structures can be found in the open and shadow processes.

6 Conclusion

Like it or not, the shadow turn in globalization is irreversible. Just like globalization in the neoliberal phase, this shadow phase is not a project by design or one that is orchestrated by an almighty state. Rather it is an interactive process in which many structural factors and agencies play a part. Nonetheless, various China-related factors and actors have been instrumental in shaping the development. In doing so, China has assumed a historical role comparable to the one once borne by the West in neoliberal globalization.

Such globalizing drive of the shadow is peculiar to our time. Unlike conventional smuggling and other transnational crimes, the dominant form of contemporary shadow exchange is mass smuggling by the common people. More importantly, the vast numbers of seemingly unrelated crowd smugglers in various regions of the world are in fact unwitting participants of a larger globalizing process, most remarkably linked by Chinese shadow networks in conjunction with local agents.

This historical process is changing the global economy in a number of ways. First, the extent of inclusion and penetration is unprecedented, resulting in an active integration of people and places across the world. Unlike mainstream globalization spearheaded by multinationals, transnational shadow exchange is carried out by millions of people, including those from poor countries, in numerous roles and capacities. The reach of this globalizing drive is unparalleled. Its implication for local development is also far-reaching.

Second, the process is reshaping existing global city networks and the locational division of labour in the world economy. Under neoliberal globalization, most of the international trade and flow of resources have taken place between established cosmopolitan cities. With the expansion of transnational shadow exchange, new networks of supplier centres, transit hubs, and distribution points have emerged. Many once-peripheral cities have become major centres of shadow trade, with emerging hierarchical orders exhibiting locational division. Global resource flow is thus no longer coordinated exclusively by a few Western metropolises.

Third, the process is redefining the global value chain. This happens when many shadow transactions are fully integrated into existing supply and distribution chains, rather than running parallel to them. In fact, the presence of shadow links in the global value chains is widely recognized by corporate actors and multinationals. Instead of seeking to eliminate these links, corporate actors have taken advantage of the flexibility and adaptability of these shadow links to advance their businesses in otherwise unfamiliar or unfriendly environments.

Fourth, just as smuggling has shaped modern state building in the past, contemporary shadow exchange is reconfiguring state power, most notably at state borders. With the proliferation of cross-border shadow activities, states are no longer dealing with occasional smugglers but are facing a huge volume of grey activities on a daily basis. State authorities are obliged to make adaptations to border governance, where delicate mechanisms of managing antagonism, conciliation, and symbiosis are developed in response to new, dynamic situations. In many instances, shadow actors and their normative practices are incorporated into the regime of control, resulting in a kind of grey governance where an informal, illicit order operates within an otherwise highly regulated space. The supposedly formalistic, despotic power of the state therefore descends into an ambiguous licit–illicit nexus in the everyday governance of shadow activities.

By integrating a wide spectrum of actors into its operations, by regrouping transnational city networks, by redefining global value chain, and by reconfiguring state power, this new phase of globalization is reshaping the historical geography of global capitalism. More importantly, this new phase of globalization is China-centred. China is a major driving force that provides the institutional infrastructure and coordinating agency. By virtue of being a manufacturer, supplier, consumer, and distributor of shadow products and services, China constitutes a central link in the shadow value chains. At the same time, its Belt and Road Initiative has provided infrastructural support as well as economic opportunity for both formal and shadow trades to take place. Many long-existing Chinese diasporic connections are creatively mobilized to form a worldwide web of shadow networks. The overall result is the formation of a global system of operations, with China positioned at the nodal centre of rhizomatic flows of shadow commodities, finance, and services.

It is obvious that China has benefited from this new globalizing drive in terms of exports, counterfeiting, industrial and technological espionage, capital transfer, and so on. Because of that, China has been assertively engaging in both dimensions of globalization: in the open process through its Belt and Road Initiative and in the clandestine process through its shadow networks. It has wasted no time to co-opt diasporic shadow networks to increase its political and economic leverage. Arguably, China's shadow power will soon become an important source of influence with its rising hegemonic position in the global shadow economy. Much closer scrutiny of this dimension of power will be needed.

References

Alff, Henryk (2016a). 'Getting Stuck within Flows: Limited Interaction and Peripheralization at the Kazakhstan-China Border'. *Central Asian Survey* 35 (3): 369–386.

Alff, Henryk (2016b). 'Flowing Goods, Hardening Borders? China's Commercial Expansion into Kyrgyzstan Re-examined'. *Eurasian Geography and Economics* 57 (3): 433–456.

Alff, Henryk (2017). 'Trading on Change Bazaars and Social Transformation in the Borderlands of Kazakhstan, Kyrgyzstan and Xinjiang'. In Martin Saxer and Juan Zhang, eds., *The Art of Neighbouring Making Relations across China's Borders*. Amsterdam: Amsterdam University Press, 95–119.

Amilhat-Szary, Anne-Laure and Frédéric Giraut, eds. (2015). *Borderities and the Politics of Contemporary Mobile Borders*. Basingstoke: Palgrave Macmillan.

Anders, Gerhard (2010). *In the Shadow of Good Governance: An Ethnography of Civil Reform in Africa*. Leiden: Brill.

Anderson, Joan B. and James Gerber (2008). *Fifty Years of Change on the U.S.-Mexico Border: Growth Development and Quality of Life*. Austin: University of Texas Press.

Andreas, Peter (2000). *Border Games: Policing the U.S.-Mexico Divide*. Ithaca: Cornell University Press.

Andreas, Peter (2004). 'Illicit International Political Economy: The Clandestine Side of Globalization'. *Review of International Political Economy* 11 (3): 641–652.

Andreas, Peter (2011). 'Illicit Globalization: Myths, Misconceptions, and Historical Lessons'. *Political Science Quarterly* 126 (3): 403–425.

Andreas, Peter (2013). *Smuggler Nation: How Illicit Trade Made America*. New York: Oxford University Press.

Andreas, Peter (2015). 'International Politics and the Illicit Global Economy'. *Perspectives on Politics* 13 (3): 782–788.

Annual Report of China Ports 中国口岸年鉴. 2018; 2019. www.tjcn.org/e/tags/?tagname=%D6%D0%B9%FA%BF%DA%B0%B6%C4%EA%BC%F8.

Apple Daily 蘋果日報. 18 May 2017; 4 July 2017; 30 March 2018.

Ayers, Ed (1996). 'The Expanding Shadow Economy'. *World Watch* 9 (4): 11–23.

Ayimpam, Sylvie (2015). 'Informal Trade, Cross Border Networks and Contraband of Asian Textiles from Brazzaville to Kinshasa'. *Journal of Borderlands Studies* 30 (3): 395–403.

Bailyn, Bernard (2005). *Atlantic History: Concept and Contours*. Cambridge, MA: Harvard University Press, 88.

Balibar, Étienne (2002). *Politics and the Other Scene*. London: Verso.

Ballvé, Teo (2012). 'Everyday State Formation: Territory, Decentralization, and the Narco Landgrab in Colombia'. *Environment and Planning D* 30: 603–622.

Baud, Michiel and Willem van Schendel (1997). 'Toward a Comparative History of Borderlands'. *Journal of World History* 8 (2): 211–242.

Beck, Ulrich (2000). *What Is Globalization?* Cambridge, MA: Polity Press.

Belguidoum, Saïd and Olivier Pleiz (2015). 'Yiwu: The Creation of a Global Market Town in China'. *Articulo – Journal of Urban Research* 12. https://doi .org/10.4000/articulo.2863.

Benjamin, Nancy, Stephen Golub, and Ahmadou Aly Mbaye (2015). 'Informality, Trade Policies and Smuggling in West Africa'. *Journal of Borderlands Studies* 30 (3): 381–394.

Bitabarova, Assel G. (2018). 'Unpacking Sino-Central Asian Engagement along the New Silk Road: A Case Study of Kazakhstan'. *Journal of Contemporary East Asia Studies* 7 (2): 149–173.

Brambilla, Chiara (2015). 'Exploring the Critical Potential of the Borderscapes Concept'. *Geopolitics* 20 (1): 14–34.

Braudel, Fernand (1992). *The Wheels of Commerce*. Berkeley, Los Angeles: University of California Press.

Bredeloup, Sylvie (2012). 'African Trading Post in Guangzhou: Emergent or Recurrent Commercial Form?' *African Diaspora* 5 (1): 27–50.

Brenner, Neil, Jamie Peck and Nik Theodore (2010). 'Variegated Neoliberalization: Geographies, Modalities, Pathways'. *Global Networks* 10 (2): 182–222.

Byrne, James, Joseph Byrne, Lucas Kuo, and Lauren Sung (2021). *Black Gold: Exposing North Korea's Oil Procurement Networks*. Washington, DC: C4ADS and RUSI.

Castells, Manuel (1998). *End of Millennium*. London: Blackwell.

Castells, Manuel and Alejandro Portes (1989). 'World Underneath: The Origins, Dynamics, and Effects of the Informal Economy'. In Alejandro Portes, Manuel Castells, and Lauren A. Benton, eds., *The Informal Economy: Studies in Advanced and Less Developed Countries*. Baltimore: Johns Hopkins University Press, 11-41.

Centeno, Miguel Angel and Alejandro Portes (2006). 'The Informal Economy in the Shadow of the State'. In Patricia Fernández-Kelly and Jon Shefner, eds., *Out of the Shadows: Political Action and the Informal Economy in Latin America*. University Park: Pennsylvania State University, 26–54.

Center for Strategic and International Studies (2023). *A Survey of Reported Chinese Espionage, 2000 to the Present*. Washington, DC: CSIS.

Chen, Yung-fa (1995). 'The Blooming Poppy under the Red Sun: The Yan'an Way and the Opium Trade'. In Tony Saich and Hans van de Ven, eds., *New Perspectives on the Chinese Communist Revolution*. New York: M.E. Sharpe, 263–298.

Cheuk, Ka-Kin (2016). 'Everyday Diplomacy among Indian Traders in a Chinese Fabric Market'. *The Cambridge Journal of Anthropology* 34 (2): 42–58.

China E- Commerce Research Centre 中国电子商务研究中心 (2010). 2010年度中国电子商务市场数据监测报告 (*China E-commerce 2010 Market Monitor Report*). http://b2b.toocle.com.

Cleaver, Frances (2015). 'In Pursuit of Arrangements that Work: Bricolage, Practical Norms and Everyday Water Government'. In Tom De Herdt and Jean-Pierre Olivier de Sardan, eds., *Real Governance and Practical Norms in Sub-Sahara Africa: The Game of the Rules*. London: Routledge, 207–227.

Cornelius, Wayne A. (2004). 'Controlling "Unwanted" Immigration: Lessons from the United States, 1993–2004'. San Diego: UCSD CCIS Working Paper 92.

De Soto, Hernando (2000). *The Mystery of Capital: Why Capitalism Triumphs in the West and Fails Everywhere Else*. New York: Basic Books.

Deleuze, Gilles and Felix Guattari, translated by Brian Massumi (1988). *A Thousand Plateaus: Capitalism and Schizophrenia*. Minneapolis, London: University of Minnesota Press.

Dell'Anno, Roberto and Friedrich Schneider (2003). 'The Shadow Economy of Italy and Other OECD Countries: What Do We Know?' *Journal of Public Finance and Public Choice* 21 (2–3): 97–120.

Economist, The. 23 June 2020.

Eilat, Yair and Clifford Zinnes (2002). 'The Shadow Economy in Transition Countries: Friend of Foe? A Policy Perspective'. *World Development* 30 (7): 1233–1254.

El Qorchi, Mohammed, Samuel Munzele Maimbo, and John F. Wilson (2003). 'Informal Funds Transfer Systems: An Analysis of the Informal Hawala System'. A Joint IMF–World Bank Paper. International Monetary Fund.

Elsing, Sarah (2019). 'Navigating Small-Scale Trade across Thai-Lao Border Checkpoints: Legitimacy, Social Relations and Money'. *Journal of Contemporary Asia* 49 (2): 216–232.

Endres, Kirsten W. (2014). 'Making Law: Small-Scale Trade and Corrupt Exceptions at the Vietnam–China Border'. *American Anthropologist* 116 (3): 611–625.

Evans, Peter (2008). 'Is an Alternative Globalization Possible?' *Politics & Society* 36 (2): 271–305.

Fedorova, Kapitolina (2012). 'Transborder Trade on the Russian–Chinese Border: Problems of Interethnic Communication'. In Bettina Bruns and Judith Miggelbrink, eds., *Subverting Borders Doing Research on Smuggling and Small-Scale Trade*. Wiesbaden: VS Verlag, 107–128.

Feenstra, Robert C. (1998). 'Integration of Trade and Disintegration of Production in the Global Economy'. *Journal of Economic Perspectives* 12 (4): 31–50.

Fehlings, Susanne (2020). 'Doing Business in Yabaolu Market, Beijing: (Inter-) ethnic Entrepreneurship, Trust and Friendship between Caucasian and Chinese Traders'. *Central Asian Survey* 39 (1): 95–115.

Fehlings, Susanne (2022). *Traders, Informal Trade and Markets between the Caucasus and China*. Singapore: Palgrave Macmillan.

Feuling, Bradley A. (2010). 'Developing China Sales and Distribution Capabilities'. *China Business Review*, 1 July. www.chinabusinessreview .com/developing-china-sales-and-distribution-capabilities/. Accessed 25 October 2015.

Fleming, Matthew H., John Roman, and Graham Farrell (2000). 'The Shadow Economy'. *Journal of International Affairs* 53 (2): 387–409.

Flynn, Donna K. (1997). '"We Are the Border": Identity, Exchange, and the State along the Benin-Nigeria Border'. *American Ethnologist* 24 (2):311–330.

Galemba, Rebecca B. (2008). 'Informal and Illicit Entrepreneurs: Fighting for a Place in the Neoliberal Economic Order'. *Anthropology of Work Review* 19 (2): 10–25.

Gel'man, Vladimir (2004). 'The Unrule of Law in the Making: The Politics of Informal Institution Building in Russia'. *Europe-Asia Studies* 56 (7): 1021–1040.

Gel'man, Vladimir (2012). 'Subversive Institutions and Informal Governance in Contemporary Russia'. In Thomas Christiansen and Christine Neuhold, eds., *International Handbook on Informal Governance*. Cheltenham: Edward Elgar, 135–153.

Gereffi, Gary (2014). 'Global Value Chains in a Post-Washington Consensus World'. *Review of International Political Economy* 21 (1): 9–37.

Gereffi, Gary, John Humphrey, and Timothy Sturgeon (2005). 'The Governance of Global Value Chains'. *Review of International Political Economy* 12 (1): 78–104. https://doi.org/10.1080/09692290500049805.

Gershuny, Jonathan I. (1979). 'The Informal Economy: Its Role in Post-Industrial Society'. *Futures* 11 (1): 3–15.

Gibson-Graham, J. K. (2006). *A Postcapitalist Politics*. Minneapolis: University of Minnesota Press.

Gilles, Angelo (2015). 'The Social Construction of Guangzhou as a Translocal Trading Place'. *Journal of Current Chinese Affairs* 44 (4): 17–47.

Gilman, Nils, Jesse Goldhammer, and Steven Weber (2013). 'Deviant Globalization'. In Michael Miklaucic and Jacqueline Brewer, eds., *Convergence: Illicit Networks and National Security in the Age of Globalization*. Washington, DC: National Defense University Press, 3–13.

Gong, Ting (2006). 'Corruption and Local Governance: The Double Identity of Chinese Local Governments in Market Reform'. *The Pacific Review* 19 (1): 85–102.

Goodman, David S. G. (1996). 'Corruption in the PLA'. In Gerald Segal and Richard H. Yang, eds., *Chinese Economic Reform: The Impact on Security*. Oxford: Routledge, 35–52.

Guangzhou Daily 廣州日報. 21 November 2007.

Hagmann, Tobias and Didier Péclard (2010). 'Negotiating Statehood: Dynamics of Power and Domination in Africa'. *Development and Change* 41 (4): 539–562.

Hall, Tim (2012). 'Geographies of the Illicit: Globalization and Organized Crime'. *Progress in Human Geography* 37 (3): 366–385.

Han, Chang-Ryung, Hans Nelen, and Yeonho Kang (2015). 'A Case Study on Shuttle Trade between Korea and China'. *Journal of Borderlands Studies* 30 (3): 437–451.

Hannas, William C., James Mulvenon and Anna B. Puglisi (2013). *Chinese Industrial Espionage: Technology Acquisition and Military Modernization*. Oxford: Routledge.

Harper, Tim and Sunil S. Amrith (2012). 'Sites of Asian Interaction: An Introduction'. *Modern Asian Studies* 46 (2): 249–257.

Harrington, Brooke (2016). *Capital without Borders: Wealth Managers and the One Percent*. Cambridge, MA: Harvard University Press.

Haugen, Heidi Østbø (2012). 'Nigerians in China: A Second State of Immobility'. *International Migration* 50 (2): 65–80.

Haugen, Heidi Østbø (2018). 'Petty Commodities, Serious Business: The Governance of Fashion Jewellery Chains between China and Ghana'. *Global Networks* 18 (2): 307–325.

Haugen, Heidi Østbø (2019a). 'China-Africa Exports: Governance Through Mobility and Sojourning'. *Journal of Contemporary Asia* 49 (2): 294–312.

Haugen, Heidi Østbø (2019b). 'Residence Registration in China's Immigration Control: Africans in Guangzhou'. In Angela Lehmann and Pauline Leonard, eds., *Destination China. Immigration to China in the Post-Reform Era*. New York: Palgrave Macmillan, 45–64.

Helmke, Gretchen and Steven Levitsky (2004). 'Informal Institutions and Comparative Politics: A Research Agenda'. *Perspectives on Politics* 2 (4): 725–740.

Herzog, Lawrence A. (1990). *Where North Meets South: Cities, Space, and Politics on the U.S.-Mexico Border*. Austin: Center for Mexican American Studies.

Heyman, Josiah McC. and Alan Smart (1999). 'States and Illegal Practices: An Overview'. In Josiah McC. Heyman, ed., *States and Illegal Practices*. Oxford: Berg, 1–24.

Hong Kong Trade Development Council (2016). 'China-Kazakhstan Border Cooperation in Xinjiang'. http://hkmb.hktdc.com/en/1X0A5JIX/hktdc-research/China-Kazakhstan-Border-Co-operation-in-Xinjiang. Accessed 30 April 2018.

Horden, Peregrine and Nicholas Purcell (2000). *The Corrupting Sea: A Study of Mediterranean History*. Oxford: Wiley-Blackwell.

Hu, Wei 胡伟 and Yu Chang 于畅 (2020). 区域协调发展战略背景下中国边境经济合作区发展研究 ('Study on China's Border Economy Cooperate Districts under the Background of Regional Coordinative Development Strategy'). 区域经济评论 (*Review of Regional Economy*) 2. www.cre.org.cn/qy/xietiao/15955.html. Accessed 29 September 2022.

Hung, Eva P. W. and Tak-Wing Ngo (2019). 'Organised Informality and Suitcase Trading in the Pearl River Delta Region'. *Journal of Contemporary Asia* 49 (2): 233–253.

Ibañez-Tirado, Diana and Magnus Marsden (2020). 'Trade "Outside the Law": Uzbek and Afghan Transnational Merchants between Yiwu and South-Central Asia'. *Central Asian Survey* 39 (1): 135–154.

ILO (2017). *Global Estimates of Modern Slavery: Forced Labour and Forced Marriage*. Geneva: ILO.

International Business Times. 21 February 2014.

Jacobs, Mark D. (2016). *Yiwu, China: A Study of the World's Largest Small Commodities Market*. New Jersey: Homa & Sekey Books.

Jeganathan, Pradeep (2018). 'Border, Checkpoint, Bodies'. In Alexander Horstmann, Martin Saxer, and Alessandro Rippa, eds., *Routledge Handbook of Asian Borderlands*. Abingdon: Routledge, 403–410.

Jin, Xin, Gideon Bolt, and Pieter Hooimeijer (2021). 'Africans in Guangzhou: Is the Ethnic Enclave Model Applicable in the Chinese Context?' *Cities* 117: 1–11.

Jung, Dietrich, ed. (2003). *Shadow Globalization, Ethnic Conflicts and New Wars: A Political Economy of Intra-State War*. London: Routledge.

Kar, Dev and Brian LeBlanc (2013). *Illicit Financial Flows from Developing Countries: 2002-2011*. Washington, DC: Global Financial Integrity.

Karras, Alan L. (2010). *Smuggling: Contraband and Corruption in World History*. Maryland: Rowman & Littlefield.

Keefe, Patrick Radden (2013). 'The Geography of Badness: Mapping the Hubs of the Illicit Global Economy'. In Michael Miklaucic and Jacqueline Brewer, eds., *Convergence: Illicit Networks and National Security in the Age of Globalization*. Washington, DC: National Defense University Press, 3–13.

Kelman, Jonathan H. C. (2015). 'States Can Play, too: Constructing a Typology of State Participation in Illicit Flows'. *Crime, Law and Social Change* 64: 37–55.

Kleine, Mareike. (2013). 'Knowing Your Limits: Informal Governance and Judgement in the EU'. *The Review of International Organizations* 8: 245–264.

Koff, Harlan (2015). 'Informal Economies in European and American Cross-border Regions'. *Journal of Borderlands Studies* 30 (3): 469–487.

Koster, Martijn and Alan Smart (2019). 'Performing In/formality beyond the Dichotomy: An Introduction'. *Anthropologica* 61: 20–24.

Kupatadze, Alexander and Lakshmi Kumar (2022). *Everything Everywhere All at Once: Understanding the Implications of the Belt and Road Initiative on Trade-Based Money Laundering (TBML) and Illicit Supply Chains*. Washington: Global Financial Integrity.

Kus, Basak (2010). 'Regulatory Governance and the Informal Economy: Cross-National Comparisons'. *Socio-Economic Review* 8 (3): 487–510.

Laine, Jussi P. (2016). 'The Multiscalar Production of Borders'. *Geopolitics* 21 (3): 465–482.

Laruelle, Marlène and Sébastien Peyrouse (2009). 'Cross-border Minorities as Cultural and Economic Mediators between China and Central Asia'. *China and Eurasia Forum Quarterly* 7 (1): 93–119.

Lo, T. Wing and Sharon Ingrid Kwok (2017). 'Triad Organized Crime in Macau Casinos: Extra-Legal Governance and Entrepreneurship'. *The British Journal of Criminology* 57 (3): 589–607.

Macau Daily 澳門日報. 17 June 2022; 2 September 2022.

Mahanty, Sango (2019). 'Shadow Economies and the State: A Comparison of Cassava and Timber Networks on the Cambodia–Vietnam Frontier'. *Journal of Contemporary Asia* 49 (2): 193–215.

Maloney, William F. (2004). 'Informality Revisited'. *World Development* 32 (7): 1159–1178.

Mandel, Robert (2010). *Dark Logic: Transnational Criminal Tactics and Global Security*. Stanford: Stanford University Press.

Marsden, Magnus (2016). 'Crossing Eurasia: Trans-regional Afghan Trading Networks in China and Beyond'. *Central Asian Survey* 35 (1): 1–15.

Marsden, Magnus (2018). 'Beyond Bukhara: Trade, Identity and Interregional Exchange across Asia'. *History and Anthropology* 29 (sup1): S84–S100.

Mathew, Johan (2016). *Margins of the Market Trafficking and Capitalism across the Arabian Sea*. Oakland, CA: University of California Press.

Mathews, Gordon (2011). *Ghetto at the Center of the World: Chungking Mansion, Hong Kong*. Hong Kong: Hong Kong University Press.

Mathews, Gordon (2015). 'Taking Copies from China Past Customs: Routines, Risks, and the Possibility of Catastrophe'. *Journal of Borderlands Studies* 30 (3): 423–435.

Mathews, Gordon, Gustavo Lins Ribeiro, and Carlos Alba Vega, eds. (2012). *Globalization from Below: The World's Other Economy*. London: Routledge.

Mathews, Gordon, Linessa Dan Lin, and Yang Yang (2017). *The World in Guangzhou: Africans and Other Foreigners in South China's Global Marketplace*. Hong Kong: Hong Kong University Press.

Meehan, Patrick and Seng Lawn Dan (2023). 'Brokered Rule: Militias, Drugs, and Borderland Governance in the Myanmar–China Borderlands'. *Journal of Contemporary Asia* 53 (4): 561–583.

Mertha, Andrew (2005). *The Politics of Piracy: Intellectual Property in Contemporary China*. Ithaca: Cornell University Press.

Ming Pao 明報. 28 October 2016.

Mitchell, Timothy (2008). 'Rethinking Economy'. *Geoforum* 39: 1116–1121.

Mizoguchi, Atsushi 溝口敦 (2016). 闇経済の怪物たち (*Monsters of the Dark Economy*). Tokyo 東京:光文社.

Møller, Henrik Kloppenborg (2021). 'Borderlines, Livelihood, and Ethnicity in the Yunnan–Myanmar Borderlands: A Rohingya Jade Trader's Narratives'. In Dan Smyer Yü and Karin Dean, eds., *Yunnan–Burma–Bengal Corridor Geographies*. London: Routledge, 122–142.

Naim, Moises (2005). *Illicit: How Smugglers, Traffickers, and Copycats Are Hijacking the Global Economy*. New York: Doubleday.

Neuwirth, Robert (2012). *Stealth of Nations: The Global Rise of the Informal Economy*. New York: Anchor Books.

Newman, David and Anssi Paasi (1998). 'Fences and Neighbors in the Postmodern World: Boundary Narratives in Political Geography'. *Progress in Human Geography* 22 (2): 186–207.

Ngo, Tak-Wing (2008). 'Rent-Seeking and Economic Governance in the Structural Nexus of Corruption in China'. *Crime, Law and Social Change* 49 (1): 27–44.

Ngo, Tak-Wing (2015). 'Asia and the Historicity of the Market Economy'. *Verge: Studies in Global Asias* 1 (1): 44–50.

Ngo, Tak-Wing (2018). 'Overcoming Institutional Voids during Market Transition: Private Sector Financing in China'. *Sociétés Politiques Compares* 44 (janvier-avril): 1–20.

Ngo, Tak-Wing (2023). 'Informal Governance in China's Borders'. In Ceren Ergenc and David S. G. Goodman, eds., *Handbook on Local Governance in China: Structures, Variations, and Innovations*. Cheltenham: Edward Elgar, 127–137.

Ngo, Tak-Wing and Eva. P. W. Hung (2019). 'The Political Economy of Border Checkpoints in Shadow Exchanges'. *Journal of Contemporary Asia* 49 (2): 178–192.

Ngo, Tak-Wing and Eva. P. W. Hung (2020). 'Introduction: Informal Exchanges and Contending Connectivity along the Shadow Silk Roads'. In Eva P. W. Hung and Tak-Wing Ngo, eds., *Shadow Exchanges along the New Silk Roads*. Amsterdam: Amsterdam University Press, 15–36.

Nicita, Alessandro and Carlos Razo (2021). 'China: The Rise of a Trade Titan'. 27 April, UNCTAD. https://unctad.org/news/china-rise-trade-titan.

Njikam, Ousmanou and Gérard Tchouassi (2011). 'Women in Informal Cross-Border Trade: Empirical Evidence from Cameroon'. *International Journal of Economics and Finance* 3 (3): 202–213.

Nordstrom, Carolyn (2000). 'Shadows and Sovereigns'. *Theory, Culture & Society* 17 (4): 35–54.

Nordstrom, Carolyn (2011). 'Extra-Legality'. *Middle East Report* 261. https://merip.org/2011/11/extra-legality/.

Ødegaard, Cecilie V. (2008). 'Informal Trade, *Contrabando* and Prosperous Socialities in Arequipa, Peru'. *Journal of Anthropology* 73 (2): 241–266.

OECD/EUIPO (2016). *Trade in Counterfeit and Pirated Goods: Mapping the Economic Impact*. Paris: OECD.

OECD/ILO (2019). *Tackling Vulnerability in the Informal Economy, Development Centre Studies*. Paris: OECD. http://doi.org/10.1787/939b7bcd-en.

Olivier de Sardan, Jean-Pierre (2015). 'Practical Norms: Informal Regulations within Public Bureaucracies (in Africa and Beyond)'. In Tom De Herdt and Jean-Pierre Olivier de Sardan, eds., *Real Governance and Practical Norms in Sub-Sahara Africa: The Game of the Rules*. London: Routledge, 19–62.

Ong, Aihwa (2004). 'The Chinese Axis: Zoning Technologies and Variegated Sovereignty'. *Journal of East Asian Studies* 4, 69–96.

Pahl. R. E. (1988). 'Some Remarks on Informal Work, Social Polarization and the Social Structure'. *International Journal of Urban and Regional Research* 12 (2): 247–267.

Parker, Noel and Rebecca Adler-Nissen (2012). 'Picking and Choosing the "Sovereign" Border: A Theory of Changing State Bordering Practices'. *Geopolitics* 17 (4): 773–796.

Parker, Noel and Nick Vaughan-Williams et al. (2009). 'Lines in the Sand? Towards an Agenda for Critical Border Studies'. *Geopolitics* 14 (3): 582–587.

Patrick, Stewart (2011). *Weak Links: Fragile States, Global Threats, and International Security*. New York: Oxford University Press.

Pengbai Xinwen 澎湃新闻. 25 July 2018.

Perry, Guillerom E., William F. Maloney, Omar S. Arias et al. (2007). *Informality: Exit and Exclusion*. Washington, DC: World Bank.

Plümmer, Franziska (2022). *Rethinking Authority in China's Border Regime*. Amsterdam: Amsterdam University Press.

Pohit, Sanjib and Nisha Taneja (2000). 'India's Informal Trade with Bangladesh and Nepal: A Qualitative Assessment'. New Delhi: Indian Council for Research on International Economic Relations Working Paper No. 58.

Portes, Alejandro and Robert L. Bach (1985). *Latin Journey: Cuban and Mexican Immigrants in the United States*. Berkeley: University of California Press.

Portes, Alejandro and Saskia Sassen-Koob (1987). 'Making It Underground: Comparative Material on the Informal Sector in Western Market Economies'. *American Journal of Sociology* 93 (1): 30–61.

Priest, George L. (1994). 'The Ambiguous Moral Foundations of the Underground Economy'. *The Yale Law Journal* 10321 (8): 2259–2288.

ProPublica. 31 July 2017; 12 July 2023

Reh, Christine (2012). 'Informal Politics: The Normative Challenge'. In Thomas Christiansen and Christine Neuhold, eds., *International Handbook on Informal Governance*. Cheltenham: Edward Elgar, 65–84.

Reporter, The 報道者. 12 July 2020; 9 January 2023.

Rumford, Chris (2012). 'Towards a Multiperspectival Study of Borders'. *Geopolitics* 17 (4): 887–902.

Sassen, Saskia (2006). 'Toward an Alternative Narrative about Globalization: Global Cities and Survival Circuits'. *Cahiers du Genre* 40 (1): 67–89.

Scheele, Judith (2012). *Smugglers and Saints of the Sahara: Regional Connectivity in the Twentieth Century*. New York: Cambridge University Press.

Schneider, Friedrich and Colin C. Williams (2013). *The Shadow Economy*. London: Institute of Economic Affairs.

Schröder, Philipp (2020). 'Business 2.0: Kyrgyz Middlemen in Guangzhou'. *Central Asian Survey* 39 (1): 116–134.

Sharman, J. C. (2011). *The Money Laundry: Regulating Criminal Finance in the Global Economy*. Ithaca: Cornell University Press.

Shelley, Louise I. (2014). *Dirty Entanglements: Corruption, Crime, and Terrorism*. New York: Cambridge University Press.

Shelley, Louise I. (2018). *Dark Commerce: How a New Illicit Economy Is Threatening Our Future. Princeton*: Princeton University Press.

Shen, Wei (2016). *Shadow Banking in China*. Cheltenham: Edward Elgar.

Sheppard, Eric (2002). 'The Spaces and Times of Globalization: Place, Scale, Networks, and Positionality'. *Economic Geography* 78 (3): 307–330.

Si, Zhenzhong, Jenelle Regnier-Davies, and Steffanie Scott (2018). 'Food Safety in Urban China: Perceptions and Coping Strategies of Residents in Nanjing'. *China Information* 32 (3): 377–399.

Smart, Alan and George Lin (2004). 'Border Management and Growth Coalitions in the Hong Kong Transborder Region'. *Identities: Global Studies in Culture and Power* 11 (3): 377–396.

Smart, Alan and Josephine Smart (2008). 'Time-Space Punctuation: Hong Kong's Border Regime and Limits on Mobility'. *Pacific Affairs* 81 (2): 175–193.

Smith, Philip M. (1997). 'Assessing the Size of the Underground Economy: The Statistics Canada Perspective'. In Owen Lippert and Michael Walker, eds., *The Underground Economy: Global Evidence of Its Size and Impact*. Vancouver: The Fraser Institute, 11–36.

Sohn, Christophe (2016). 'Navigating Borders' Multiplicity: The Critical Potential of Assemblage'. *Area* 48 (2): 183–189.

Spector, Regine A. (2017). *Order at the Bazaar: Power and Trade in Central Asia*. Ithaca: Cornell University Press.

Strange, Susan (1996). *The Retreat of the State: The Diffusions of Power in the World Economy.* Cambridge: Cambridge University Press.

Su, Xiaobo (2018). 'Fragmented Sovereignty and the Geopolitics of Illicit Drugs in Northern Burma'. *Political Geography* 63: 20–30.

Sugita, Yoneyuki (2019). 'China's Food Safety Problems and the Establishment of a Dual Economy: A Case of Vegetables'. In Victor Teo and Sungwon Yoon, eds., *Illicit Industries and China's Shadow Economy: Challenges and Prospects for Global Governance and Human Security.* London: Routledge, 65–77.

Sur, Malini (2013). 'Through Metal Fences: Material Mobility and the Politics of Transnationality at Borders'. *Mobilities* 8 (1): 70–89.

Suzuki, Tomo (2007a). 'Accountics: Impacts of Internationally Standardized Accounting on the Japanese Socio-economy'. *Accounting, Organizations and Society* 32: 263–301.

Suzuki, Tomo (2007b). 'A History of Japanese Accounting Reforms as a Microfoundation of the Democratic Socio-economy: Accountics Part II'. *Accounting, Organizations and Society* 32: 543–575.

Tagliacozzo, Eric (2005). *Secret Trades, Porous Borders Smuggling and States along a Southeast Asian Frontier, 1865–1915*. New Haven: Yale University Press.

Teo, Victor and Sungwon Yoon (2019). 'Illicit Industries and China's Shadow Economy: Challenges and Prospects for Global Governance and Human Security'. In Victor Teo and Sungwon Yoon, eds., *Illicit Industries and China's Shadow Economy: Challenges and Prospects for Global Governance and Human Security*. London: Routledge, 1–28.

Thai, Philip (2018). *China's War on Smuggling: Law, Economic Life, and the Making of the Modern State*, 1842–1965. New York: Columbia University Press.

Thoumi, Francisco E. (2005). 'The Numbers Game: Let's All Guess the Size of the Illegal Drug Industry!' *Journal of Drug Issues* 35 (Winter): 185–200.

Tienda, Marta and Rebecca Raijman (2000). 'Immigrants' Income Packaging and Invisible Labor Force Activity'. *Social Science Quarterly* 81 (1): 291–310.

Tomisaka, Satoshi 富坂聰 (2010). 中国の地下経済 (*China's Underground Economy)*. Tokyo 東京: 文藝春秋.

Tsai, Kellee S. (2002). *Back-Alley Banking: Private Entrepreneurs in China*. Ithaca: Cornell University Press.

United States Chamber of Commerce (2016). *Measuring the Magnitude of Global Counterfeiting*. Washington, DC: Global Intellectual Property Center.

United States Trade Representative (2011). *Review of Notorious Markets*. https://ustr.gov/sites/default/files/uploads/gsp/speeches/reports/2011/Notorious%20Markets%20List%20FINAL.pdf. Accessed 1 October 2022.

UNODC (2018). *Global Study on Smuggling of Migrants*. New York: United Nations Publication, Sales No. E.18.IV.9.

Van Schendel, Willem (2005). 'Spaces of Engagement: How Borderlands, Illegal Flows and Territorial States Interlock'. In Willem van Schendel and Itty Abraham, eds., *Illicit Flows and Criminal Things: States, Borders and the Other Side of Globalization*. Bloomington: Indiana University Press, 38–68.

Van Schendel, Willem (2020). 'Fragmented Sovereignty and Unregulated Flows: The Bangladesh–China–India–Myanmar Corridor'. In Eva P. W. Hung and Tak-Wing Ngo, eds., *Shadow Exchanges along the New Silk Road*. Amsterdam: Amsterdam University Press, 37–73.

Varese, Federico (2015). 'Underground Banking and Corruption'. In Susan Rose-Ackerman and Paul Lagunes, eds., *Greed, Corruption, and the Modern State: Essays in Political Economy*. Cheltenham and Northampton: Edward Elgar, 336–358.

Waldinger, Roger and Michael Lapp (1993). 'Back to the Sweatshop or Ahead to the Informal Sector?' *International Journal of Urban and Regional Research* 17 (1): 6–29.

Walker, Andrew (1999). *The Legend of the Golden Boat: Regulation, Trade, and Traders in the Borderlands of Laos, China, Thailand and Burma*. Richmond, Surrey: Curzon Press.

Walther, Olivier (2009). 'A Mobile Idea of Space. Traders, Patrons and the Cross-Border Economy in Sahelian Africa'. *Journal of Borderlands Studies* 24 (1): 34–46.

Wang, Peng (2017). *The Chinese Mafia: Organized Crime, Corruption, and Extra-Legal Protection*. Oxford: Oxford University Press.

Wank, David L. (2009). 'Local State Takeover as Multiple Rent Seeking in Private Business'. In Tak-Wing Ngo and Yongping Wu, eds., *Rent Seeking in China*. London: Routledge, 79–97.

Wedeman, Andrew (2022). 'The Dynamics and Trajectory of Corruption in Contemporary China'. *China Review* 22 (2): 21–48.

Williams, Phil (1997). 'Transnational Organized Crime and National and International Security: A Global Assessment". In Virginia Gamba, ed., Society under Siege: Crime, Violence and Illegal Weapons. South Africa: Institute for Security Studies.

Wong, Rebecca W. Y. (2021). 'Shadow Operations in Wildlife Trade under China's Belt and Road Initiative'. *China Information* 35 (2): 201–218.

Woods, Kevin (2019). 'Rubber out of the Ashes: Locating Chinese Agribusiness Investments in "Arm Sovereignties" in the Myanmar–China Borderlands'. *Territory, Politics, Governance* 7 (1): 79–95.

World Tourism Alliance (2019). *WTA Data Analysis Report of China's Inbound Tourism*. Hangzhou.

Yan, Qingmin 阎庆民 and Li Jianhua 李建华 (2014). 中国影子银行监管研究 (*A Study on the Supervision of Shadow Banking in China)*. Beijing 北京: 中国人民大学出版社.

Zhang, Shu Guang (2001). *Economic Cold War: American's Embargo against China and the Sino-Soviet Alliance*, 1949–1963. Stanford: Stanford University Press.

Zook, Matthew A. (2003). 'Underground Globalization: Mapping the Space of Flows of the Internet Adult Industry'. *Environment and Planning A* 35: 1261–1286.

Zucman, Gabriel (2013). 'The Missing Wealth of Nations: Are Europe and the U.S. Net Debtors or Net Creditors?' *The Quarterly Journal of Economics* 128 (3): 1321–1364.

Acknowledgements

This study puts together some of my findings in the past years about transnational shadow exchange. Although being marginalized in mainstream perceptions, shadow exchange constitutes a very substantial proportion of national and global economies. This phenomenon has caught the attention of an emerging community of scholars. Building on their insights, this study explores the activity from a political economy perspective and argues that a broader historical process is unfolding, giving rise to a global system of shadow exchange.

Exploring alternative modes of material value exchange and the concomitant logics of governance proves to be tedious and time-consuming, because it requires deep inquiry into hidden practices beneath the institutional façade of rules and policies. In the course of my inquiry, I have accumulated many debts to institutions and individuals who extended their help in one way or another. Funding support for the project is from the Hong Kong Research Grant Council (Ref.: UGC/FDS12(14)/H02/14; UGC/IIDS14/H01/16; and UGC/FDS14/H09/17). Some of the findings have been presented in workshops, conferences, and guest seminars in Bishkek, Chiang Mai, Colombo, Hong Kong, Kathmandu, Leiden, New York, Macao, Singapore, Suzhou, and Tokyo. I am grateful to the participants for their invaluable input.

Special thanks to Eva Hung, my research collaborator who has undertaken numerous joint fieldwork. A number of colleagues have either joined the fieldtrips, assisted in their logistical set-ups, or helped make local contacts. They include Olga Adams, Karen Chan, Xuan Dong, Lang Gao, Haknazar Hallygylyjov, Felix Lam, Hai Thanh Luong, Ngai Pun, Yelena Sadovskaya, Danielle Tan, Stan Wong, Cunyi Yin, Adeline Zhang, and Ivan Zuenko. Their indispensable help is highly appreciated. I am particularly indebted to the informants who have unreservedly shared their insider knowledge and sensitive information.

Over the years, many friends and colleagues have generously shared insights and findings with me. While too numerous to name here, some deserve special mention, most notably Richard Boyd, Jean-Pierre Cabestan, Carolyn Cartier, Sarah Elsing, Ceren Ergenç, Susanne Fehlings, Amy Freedman, David Goodman, Leo van Grunsven, Heidi Østbø Haugen, Susann Handke, Hasan Karrar, Francisco Leandro, Joseph Lee, Linda Chelan Li, Sango Mahanty, Miguel Martinez, Gordon Mathews, Anton Nikolotov, Pál Nyiri, Gijsbert Oonk, Elisa Oreglia, Frans-Paul van der Putten, Alessandro Rippa, Christopher Szabla, Willem van Schendel, Alan Smart, Josephine Smart, Alvin So, Mariko Tanigaki, Federico Varese, Jianhua Xu, and Akbar Zaidi.

Finally, Theodore Charm, Cheung Fung Fan, Leo Leung, and Morgan Mou have provided tireless assistance in various stages of data collection and background search. The final manuscript has benefited from the constructive inputs of Cambridge University Press series editor Ching Kwan Lee. Her patience and support for the project is much appreciated. Gina Rozario and Rebecca Chan have edited earlier drafts of the manuscript. To all these people and institutions, I offer my heartfelt gratitude.

Cambridge Elements

Global China

About the Series

The Cambridge Elements series Global China showcases thematic, region- or country-specific studies on China's multifaceted global engagements and impacts. Each title, written by a leading scholar of the subject matter at hand, combines a succinct, comprehensive and up-to-date overview of the debates in the scholarly literature with original analysis and a clear argument. Featuring cutting edge scholarship on arguably one of the most important and controversial developments in the 21st century, the Global China Elements series will advance a new direction of China scholarship that expands China Studies beyond China's territorial boundaries.

Cambridge Elements

Global China

Elements in the Series

Chinese Soft Power
Maria Repnikova

The Hong Kong-China Nexus
John Carroll

Clash of Empires
Ho-fung Hung

Global China as Method
Ivan Franceschini and Nicholas Loubere

Hong Kong: Global China's Restive Frontier
Ching Kwan Lee

China and Global Food Security
Shaohua Zhan

China in Global Health: Past and Present
Mary Augusta Brazelton

Global China's Shadow Exchange
Tak-Wing Ngo

A full series listing is available at: www.cambridge.org/EGLC.

For EU product safety concerns, contact us at Calle de José Abascal, 56–1°, 28003 Madrid, Spain or eugpsr@cambridge.org.

www.ingramcontent.com/pod-product-compliance
Ingram Content Group UK Ltd.
Pitfield, Milton Keynes, MK11 3LW, UK
UKHW022146080726
473066UK00010B/792

* 9 7 8 1 1 0 8 9 7 2 1 7 8 *